EXPLORING THE SEA

**An introduction to marine
biology and ocean science**

EXPLORING THE SEA

An introduction to marine biology and ocean science

by John Christopher Fine

Plexus Publishing, Inc.

Contents

Introduction

Looking out from shore, the ocean is perceived in blue or green. The vast horizon of water holds many mysteries. The selection of pictures and text chosen for these pages represents a cross section of life in the oceans; of life that depends on and surrounds the sea. While the pictures attempt to convey an appreciation for the beauty of underwater marine life and their relationships, the text is intended to be an introduction to the disciplines that have grown up around ocean science.

It is my hope that the variety of material chosen will encourage the reader to pursue knowledge about specific areas. By opening the doors to this ocean world, perhaps that curiosity can be stimulated to bring others to the sea to explore, enjoy, and appreciate.

For just as we are not all fishermen or divers, oceanographers or scientists, we are not all concerned with the same specific oceanographic or environmental issues. As a source book, as an introductory reference for the student, as a means of rediscovery for the diver or boating enthusiast, or as a photographic album that can be opened anytime to reveal the magic of life in the oceans, this book offers a general overview of the variety and splendor of the ocean realm; its fragile balance and its wonders in the deep.

There are many mansions in the sea, kingdoms under this ocean realm glowing with the magic of creation. This cyan majesty is the fountainhead of life, an orient of color, of wonders and great works.

While nations could disappear in deep sea canyons, the oceans also provide homes for the minutest specks of life. Though waves and great sea squalls destroy whole fleets, these depths contain the most delicate of beings. As leviathan and great sea creatures cavort in public view, their existence is irrevocably linked to beings that are hardly visible at all.

As we are learning constantly, there is a simple harmony in nature. People are often surprised when they come to realize that life in the wild is not simply the "endless battle for survival," played out by vicious beasts prowling the forests or haunting the oceans. There is the perpetual competition for limited habitats, for food, for mates, the perennial predator-prey relationships. But for anyone who has taken the time to observe the interaction of creatures in their natural environment, there is, more than anything else, a sense of harmony. It is this gentle harmony in nature that enables the strong and weak to strike a fair balance for survival.

Once thought limitless, the resources of the seas and oceans are continually being depleted. In many cases, the resource beds and ocean habitats themselves are being destroyed by pollution, careless and deliberate abuse, and often purposeful ruin. We have acquired the skills and technology necessary to make short shrift of these dwindling resources, while we are only beginning to develop the skills and technology necessary to expand the oceans' ability to support life, to create habitats on the ocean floor, and to view the oceans in the same way that we've come to view the land—a resource capable of depletion but also capable of being restored and husbanded.

The pictures and text that follow are aimed at presenting the continuity, the harmony in nature's underwater world that makes life beneath the sea such a fascination to behold. Perhaps by understanding the relationships between marine creatures, we can become sensitive to their importance in the interdependent chain of life and emphasize the need to develop an international atmosphere for ocean husbandry, artificial habitat construction, and conservation.

1

Large and Venerable Creatures

SHARKS

Stan Waterman, the man sitting opposite me, had filmed a general release major motion picture, *Blue Water, White Death* in 1970, documenting the pursuit of the great white shark. His friend and neighbor, Peter Benchley, inspired by Stan's films of shark behavior, and only slightly trepid after reading his own more recent accounts, agreed to participate in Stan's newest shark venture. They would voyage from home in Princeton, New Jersey to the Pacific and Indian Oceans to produce a television documentary aptly called *The Author Meets Jaws*.

Up to this point in time, Peter Benchley had never seen a great white shark. Reluctantly, Benchley agreed to dive with Stan to film the great white if they could find one. Stan Waterman who had done the underwater cinematography for Benchley's more recent oceanic adventure, *The Deep*, in 1977 was now recounting how he introduced Peter Benchley to jaws in the deep, as well as discussing aspects of shark behavior.

In the quiet moments between Stan's puffing on his pipe, I caught up on my note taking and asked him wistfully whether he was really fulfilling a valid purpose in depicting the violent aspect of shark behavior on film. We had both been diving long enough among sharks to respect their potential for violence, but also to appreciate Jacques Cousteau's offhand comment that in nature man is one of the few creatures that kills for reasons other than his own survival.

I plied Stan Waterman with such homilies as, "It seems akin to what a lion tamer does in the circus, to stimulate violence in order to create vicarious thrills in an audience attracted to danger." Rather than being miffed at my impertinence, Stan sat back pensively in his chair and nodded.

"You know, my wife has said the same thing. She abhors the depiction of violence, preferring instead my films where I can show the gentleness and beauty of nature." Then Stan removed his pipe and became the successful box office pragmatist once more. He said: "But you see people are attracted to the potential of danger. The aspect of danger brings them in. And even though we must artificially stimulate this aspect of shark behavior to capture it on film, it is really the potential of death to the divers that brings in the audience."

While shark behavior in the wild is never totally predictable, it does fall into patterns which, when understood, give the experienced diver or naturalist a sense of their body language.

Stan's conversation reminded me of a job I did translating a series of signs for my friend Serge Arnoux so he could post them in his hotel on the Pacific Atoll of Rangiroa. The signs read: "Spear fishing is not recommended as it alters the normal pacific behavior of our sharks."

That non sequitur was certainly proved out when I, like Stan, set about stimulating the violent aspect of shark behavior in the Pacific off Rangiroa in order to capture the excitement on film.

The pass through the reef was tranquil, placid. Normal fish life paid little attention to me or the two safety divers with me. There were no sharks visible on the reef. We chose a position among the coral that gave us a vantage point overlooking a flat rocky plateau. When I signaled I was ready, one of the Tahitian divers aimed his speargun at a small reef fish and fired. The fish was hit squarely. There was very little blood. The dying fish vibrated and churned on the spear. Benoit, the Tahitian diver, moved quickly, but not fast enough. In the next instant, two dozen sharks appeared over the reef and began to converge on the speared fish. Benoit let go of the spear and retreated to our coral ledge where I was filming the events. It was over in an instant. Except for a few curious sharks which arrived late and were still circling to see if there was anything left, the reef had returned to normal.

With film left, waiting until all the sharks lost interest and disappeared from sight, I motioned for Benoit to repeat the spearing. This time I signaled for him to place the speared fish under the rocks on the plateau below. The Tahitian diver complied. He speared a larger reef fish just over the rocky ledge, pushed the spear through the fish, and fixed the line into the rocks. No sooner had Benoit retreated than sharks were over the reef. This time there must have been more than a hundred of them including large black and white tips.

The behavior pattern that emerged now was typical of a shark feeding frenzy. The larger sharks began circling the speared fish and the rocks against which we pressed to observe the melee. The predators' interest was keenly on the speared fish. A large black tip lunged in, bumped the speared fish once, passing by, then whirled back on itself, apparently satisfied that the speared fish was food and fair game. The black tip lunged at the fish, taking it in its mouth. The shark shook its large head back and forth, pulling a chunk out of the fish, unable to carry it off whole because of the line holding it to the rocks. In another instant two, three, then more sharks were on the speared fish. With the same tearing motions the fish was devoured.

The feeding activity of the frenzied sharks attracted others of all sizes and description. They turned their interest toward us, began circling and closing. One especially bold, small shark, not more than 3 feet long, came in towards me and had to be bumped away. The modest effort of swimming up toward the small shark and bumping it with my camera caused it to retreat. The rest of the sharks drew further back but kept circling. With the sharks in this agitated state, we carefully surfaced, regained the boat quickly, and left the water.

We had artificially altered the normal pattern of the reef to be able to observe the competitive feeding behavior of sharks. On a similar reef, I encountered a large white tip shark. It was swimming alone. No one was spearing fish and I approached the shark head on. The shark seeing me approach swam forward curiously, then at the discharge of my camera strobe light, veered toward a large coral head, and swam under its ledge, obviously trying to get away. I did not crowd the shark, avoiding the impression of aggression which could alter the shark's normal behavior pattern in the circumstances. I shot frame after frame as the large creature looked, inspected, then avoided me. In a normal sea encounter this reaction was typical. The feeding frenzy seen in shark films, like those I was discussing with Stan Waterman, were artificially created attempts to capture the violence of animal competition for food, transferring that to danger to divers in the water.

The feeding frenzy, rarely seen in the wild, had to be stimulated.

Analysis of shark attacks on humans seems to indicate that they follow a pattern. Divers or fishermen spearing fish, often trailing them in the water are subject to attack. Divers have been attacked when pursuring a shark that was swimming away trying to avoid them. Swimmers have been attacked in murky water, often after splashing on the surface. Attacks that had no rational explanation in terms of the animals' behavior pattern were extremely rare.

Statistics kept by the U.S. Navy and the Smithsonian Institution's International Shark Attack File, a documentary compilation of some 1652 incidents involving sharks attacking humans since the 16th century, show that the majority of attacks occurred against swimmers in shallow water, near shore. The shark attack file lists 39 species as attacking man. The file documents 32 attacks by the great white shark and 27 by the tiger shark. The vast majority of the 250 species of modern sharks are considered not aggressive toward man.

Evolving more than 100 million years ago, sharks still living range in size from only a few inches to 60 feet. These larger sharks, the whale and basking shark, subsist on diets of plankton and are gentle creatures. The largest great white shark on record, by comparison, weighed some 6000 pounds and measured 21 feet long.

Sharks are cartilafinous fishes in the class Chondrichthes. They have remained virtually unchanged in evolution since creation, so well adapted are they to their predatory existence. Without bones, the shark is particularly vulnerable to internal injury. Even when a sport fisherman releases a shark after hooking it and then reeling it in to the boat, it is usually doomed, having injured its internal organs in the fight. Sharks have evolved without the air bladders that exist in most fishes to give them buoyancy. Thus, except for some species that are able to trap air in their stomachs, sharks must continually swim about to keep from sinking.

It was this lack of an air bladder that gave rise to scientists' early theories that sharks never sleep. While still the subject of a number of theories, many divers have observed sharks resting in caves, perhaps taking advantage of currents to cause water to circulate over their gills.

The sharks reproductive system is particularly interesting. Most fish discharge sperm and ova into the water, trusting to chance and statistics to fertilize sufficient numbers of eggs to insure survival of the species. In all cases, sharks copulate with the male's claspers penetrating the female to insure internal fertilization. Although

4

fertilized internally, the species bear their young diversely, either oviparously, laying eggs in a caselike sac as the whale shark does, or vivparously, with the young developing, growing, and remaining in the female's womb until birth as with the white tip or hammerhead, or as in the case of makos and threshers, ovoviviparously, where the female hatches the eggs inside her body where the young then mature until released by the female.

When finally born, the young sharks are fully equipped miniatures of their parents. They develop teeth that grow in circular rows from their gums. Some species of sharks have as many as 20 rows of teeth. As the animal grows, the teeth fall out or are used and drop out, being continually replaced by progressive rows of teeth coming in behind. One team of scientists estimated that a mature tiger shark produces 15,000 to 25,000 teeth over ten years' growth.

The shark, Jacques Cousteau said, is "the oldest killer, armed for the fray of existence in the beginning." It is the shark's instinct to survive that impels its action, its fearsome killing power only incidental to survival and not an end in itself. Anthropomorphic qualities of revenge, vengeance, meanness or purposeful stalking of human prey cannot be assigned to the sharks primitive instinctive behavior.

The shark's eye, often the subject of study by scientists trying to determine whether sharks respond to colors or patterns, has been found to be quite myopic. Although possessing a sense of smell able to detect blood in minute concentrations over distances of some 500 yards, the shark's principal sensing organ consists of nerve endings that are set in liquid-filled channels running to the outer skin. These pores along the shark's lateral line and face transmit vibrations in the water to the shark's brain. This highly sensitive "hearing" system explains how the sharks in Rangiroa responded so quickly to the agonies of the speared fish flapping at the end of the arbalette. Since the sharks were out of sight, and certainly could not have seen the fish, and since the small amount of blood produced did not even begin to migrate away from the site before the sharks appeared, it left the conclusion that the sharks extremely sensitive "hearing" system picked up the vibrations coming from the speared fish, enabling them to home in on it.

While it was once thought that pilot fish, often seen swimming alongside or in front of oceanic sharks, served to guide the short-sighted sharks to their prey, this theory has been discounted. Remora, which hang on larger fish, rays, and sharks as well as pilot fish which swim with these larger species, serve a useful function of eating

5

parasites from the sharks integument and derive the ancillary benefit of feeding on the leavings when the larger fish hunts.

RAYS AND SKATES

Rays and skates belong to the same class as sharks. They are cartilagenous fishes, with gills on the underside of their body below the pectoral fin. The largest of the rays is the manta whose graceful wings can span 20 feet from tip to tip. Large mantas weigh as much as 2 tons. The manta ray has been called "devilfish," perhaps out of superstition or fear. The harmless manta, a plankton feeding creature that is in fact quite docile and nonaggressive, has been relentlessly taunted by man. Finding it amusing sport, boatmen often harpoon the hapless creatures, thrilling themselves as the wounded manta tries to flee, pulling their boat through the water leashed by a line attached to the harpoon.

The graceful manta has no defense against man, and while there are fictional accounts of mantas descending on divers and smothering them, there have never been any authenticated accounts of actual harm to man by these large but gentle plankton feeders.

Related to the manta but possessing a barb and poison gland along their tails, are the sting rays. Sting rays are not aggressive, but have caused frequent accidents to bathers or fishermen stepping on them in shallow water or trying to free them from their nets.

Rays are capable of a variety of camouflage techniques. They bury themselves in the sand and use protective coloration. In some species, chromatophores in the skin can change color. Like sharks, rays reproduce by physical copulation. They feed on mollusks and sea shells. Some species like the spotted eagle ray are able to break into shellfish with a horny nose. Some varieties of rays such as the torpedo, are capable of generating an electric current. While the current is not enough to kill a human, they are best left alone and observed at a distance.

Skates, which are entirely harmless, closely resemble rays, save for their elongated faces. The curious pods often found along beaches with long stiff protrusions extending from all four corners are invariably skate egg pods.

CETACEANS

Marine mammals or cetaceans are among the largest creatures on

Earth. Perhaps because of their ominous size, some species have been hunted near to extinction, long after their economic value has made the hunt untenable. The syndrome that brought droves of kill-crazy hunters onto the American western plains after buffalo or to the African veldt to fell large creatures like the elephant for "sport" as well as the traffic in poached goods such as ivory, in some way at least gives one some understanding of the senseless human pillage and pursuit of cetaceans. These large creatures challenge man's need to approach danger, akin to Stan Waterman's observation about his shark thrill audiences.

Yet the tragedy that has resulted from writings and films portraying sperm whales sinking ships and killer whales stalking human prey has been a distortion of the gentleness of these great sea creatures and their keen intelligence.

The orca or killer whale is perhaps the most intelligent animal on Earth next to man. Scientists and psychologists now rate the orca as exceeding the great apes in brain power. Tom Otten, curator for mammals at Marineland of the Pacific told me once, "Working with a killer whale is like working with another person." At first blush that is a rather startling observation about a 14,000-pound creature possessing an awesome row of teeth. However, the more researchers have come to observe and work with killer whales, the more they come to understand and respect these warm-blooded sea mammals.

"The market has become a lot more sophisticated," Tom Otten said, describing the more than 1 million persons who visit Marineland each year. "They don't call them fish so much any more. They are more ecologically oriented than four or five years ago. People come here and want to be entertained, but want to go home knowing something."

Marineland's assistant curator Tim Desmond echoed Tom's observations, "The audience is more concerned and conscientious," he told me as we discussed the behavioral training of Marineland's two adult orcas.

The startling fact, perhaps the most tragic of modern times, is that man has relentlessly pursued the orca and other large marine mammals without fully understanding the extent of their intelligence and relationship to human life.

Tom's remark that people "don't call them fish so much any more," was significant. As long as a proportion of the human population considered these marine mammals fish, they were put into the category of food or strange curiosities from the ocean that represent no continuity to creation and man. Gorillas and other great apes, even

7

Killer whale or Orca performs at Marineland of the Pacific

those living in remote areas, are terrestrial and thus more accessible, more identifiable as air-breathing, live-bearing, breast-feeding, intelligent mammals in many ways akin to man. Less significant to the undiscriminating were the sea mammals, which were pushed into a psychological void by many who thought of all things in the seas and oceans as fish: slimy, slippery, flapping fish that one catches on a pole, eats, but most likely throws away after the fun of catching is over, not worthy of much consideration beyond that.

The orca thinks, reasons, expresses emotion, has personality, communicates in a complex language not fully understood by man, has a need for companionship, and, at least in confinement, has a need for human companionship and friendship.

It is difficult to study cetaceans like the orca in the wild. The incisive behavioral studies like those done under National Geographic Society grants on great apes are not possible in the remote and harsh seas where the orca lives. Studying whales in captivity is like studying gorillas in a zoo cage. One can only extrapolate theories so far in considering their place in the wild.

Laws have been passed to protect cetaceans. The Federal Marine Mammal Protection Act of 1972, prohibits the collection of whales, seals, dolphins, or other cetacea without special permits. But the most important changes are attitudinal. Slowly, human concepts and public opinion are, through education and understanding, becoming sympathetic to the plight of these intelligent marine mammals.

Bill Samaras, past president of the American Cetacean Society, touched on this aspect of increasing human awareness and sensitivity when he told me, "Now people care about whales being harpooned in the sea. Now it is not a killer whale, it's something people can identify with. When the guy captured Shamu, everybody went along with it. Recently in Vancouver they caught another killer whale and people wanted to lynch them."

Many aspects of the orca's behavior can only be understood in the light of reasoning power on a higher plane akin to man's. Marineland's Mammal Curator emphasized that above all else.

Numerous stories were recounted dealing with the orca's special relationships to their human trainers. Quick to learn, Tom Otten described his relationship with Orky, Marineland's male killer whale. "Sometimes he's five steps ahead of us and sometimes he gets bored with us and just does it on his own. Sometimes he won't put a new behavior in the show right away," Tom explained, describing how the killer whale decides when he thinks the trainer is ready to use the new trick or behavior pattern before the Marineland audience.

The killer whales in captivity at Marineland actually seek out human company and companionship. On occasion Orky has purposefully kept a trainer in the tank, gently taking the trainer's foot in its mouth to prevent the trainer leaving.

Otten's daily contact with the killer whales has resulted in a special insight into their behavior. "An animal like Orky," Tom explained, "can basically tell the mood of a person...little things he'd do. The way he'd look at you or vocalize. I hired one trainer who was afraid of killer whales. We had an agreement he wouldn't work killer whales. One day I was short of trainers. He agreed to do the show with Orky. Orky wouldn't let him down on the platform. He snapped his jaws and began blowing water," Tom explained. Apparently Orky sensed the internal feelings of the substitute trainer.

9

Tom continued to describe the extra sense these animals seem to have. "For example," Tom emphasized, "this conversation with you, I may not like it, I may not like you; if that were true and I didn't want to communicate it, I could hide my emotions and you wouldn't know my real feelings. These animals are able to sense it. That's why we're concerned with their husbandry, their well being and social behavior, their psychological well being and how we approach training, being sensitive to it," Tom continued with a kind of straightforward sincerity, that one could only translate as coming from a man who loved and respected the animals in his care. Tom smiled, reflecting, "Sometimes it's hard to figure out where they're coming from and what they want. Working with Orky is like a chess game," he admitted.

Diving off the island of **Lanai** in Hawaii, I came across about a hundred dolphin frolicking in the warm water. As I approached the shy creatures, one group of about eight broke off from the rest. I could hear the high-pitched noises the dolphin used to communicate as I dove down to photograph them. I stayed with the smaller group, snorkling on the surface as they contented themselves with my presence. Intent on taking my pictures, I lost track of direction. I became aware of two different and distinct sets of communications emitted from the dolphin underwater. The smaller group I was following made consistent noises. They were close. I could distinguish their sounds from the others. The second group of dolphin noises came from a long distance. The dolphin making these other sounds were not visible to me in the clear Hawaiian water.

The eight dolphin I was following swam rather slowly underwater, continually emitting sounds which appeared to be answered by sounds of a different pitch and nature coming from the unseen distance. Eventually, the small group of dolphin changed direction, new and different sounds were emitted back and forth until, as I swam along on top of them at the surface, the original, larger band became visible. The eight dolphin I was following rejoined the main band and the separate sounds stopped. The dolphin sounds were clearly an underwater language of sorts.

Dolphin use their high-pitched noises to home in on objects underwater. The principle works in the same way sonar or echo location works. A sound is emitted, it strikes an object underwater and bounces back. This echo location enables dolphin and orca to navigate underwater and locate prey.

A dolphin matures sexually at about eight years. They live to about thirty. Like all sea mammals they are air breathing, surfacing to expel and take in air through their blow holes. After a year gestating, the mother nurses her pup for about nine months on milk generated in her mammary glands. There is a strong parental tie and gregarious clan protectiveness for dolphin young.

Study has shown that dolphin, orca, and whales engage in a great deal of touching behavior, feeling and caressing. Experimentation has clearly shown that dolphin are able to reason at a high plane.

In attempts to understand decompression sickness occurring in human divers, scientists have studied the dolphin. Readily diving to depths of 300 feet, some have been recorded as deep as 1000 feet. While these extreme depths are abnormal for the dolphin, research has shown that these air-breathing mammals absorb oxygen more quickly than humans, storing it in musculature.

In man, the build up of carbon dioxide triggers the desire to breathe, an experience every snorkler has had diving underwater. Some snorklers attempt to rid their system of carbon dioxide by hyper-ventilating, breathing deeply two or three times before diving down. Hyperventilation is fraught with the risk of causing an oxygen debt in man, suppressing the carbon dioxide signal to the brain that triggers the breathing impulse. The oxygen debt can result in shallow water blackout as a human diver surfaces and the partial pressure of oxygen is reduced. In the dolphin, their nervous system has been found to be less sensitive to carbon dioxide than the humans. The dolphin's heartbeat slows considerably when they dive, and it has been found that the dolphin's system can tolerate an oxygen debt.

One of the problems experienced by human free divers attempting to break the world breath-holding records for depth, has been lung squeeze. The weight of the water, increasing with depth, causes pressure. This pressure squeezes the free diver's lungs. World champion free diver Enzio Mallorca was forced to come up from a depth of 86 meters, but not for lack of air, but rather the excruciating pain caused by lung squeeze. The same squeeze occurs to the free diving, breath-holding dolphin. The dolphin's lungs however are well adapted to their aquatic existence and are not harmed when collapsed by squeeze exerted from pressure at depth.

Whales, largest of the sea mammals, are among the gentlest creatures in the sea. Swimming among them with only mask and fins, one is impressed by their lithe movements. It seems extraordinary that such large creatures could be so graceful underwater, yet their movements are gainly and to some observers, poetic in motion.

Swimming among a variety of whales, approaching them in small fragile boats, I've found for the most part that these large gentle

11

creatures are almost shy. In the water I've observed whales to exhibit the utmost care to avoid hurting a diver swimming nearby. Slandered by hundreds of years of tall whaling tales of danger and adventure, of men in little wooden boats with hand-thrown harpoons, the whale is depicted in word and picture tipping over ships and drowning men. Pursued near to extinction with spotter planes guiding iron ships, automatic harpoon cannons poised in their bows, the plight of these great sea creatures was recently made even more graphic. In a film on whaling, a harpooned female was shown rolling over in death, her blood and mother's milk mixing in the sea as the iron catchers buoyed her off and went after other quarry. The dying whale's nursing calf left, a fearful and frenzied witness to his mother's last violent death throes.

Whales communicate. Researchers have recently developed a computerized pattern of whale sounds indicating what appears to be complex speech. These most recent scientific efforts analyze the whale sounds over many hours of recordings causing the researchers to conclude that the patterns can only be interpreted as a kind of whale language. The recordings show a means of communication more complex than simple sounds or noises. Diving with whales one is almost immediately taken by these amazing undersea songs, the gentle character of these behemoths and their close family instincts.

The ninety existing species of whales can be classified into two major categories: baleen (or whalebone) like the blue whale and toothed whales like the sperm whale. The baleen whales are the largest of the species; the blue whale measures 100 feet or more and can weigh as much as 120 tons. Sperm whale teeth often grace the collector's mantle, worked in scrimshaw.

As the blue whale swims through krill rich waters of its Antarctic home, the long fine plates of baleen attached to the roof of the animal's mouth act as a sieve or strainer. With each gulp, tons of the small shrimplike krill disappear into the whale's stomach. Once digested, krill provide protein and food reserves which the whales store under their skin as blubber. In the autumn of the year, the great blue whales begin their annual migration northward to warmer climes. Autumn signals the onset of the breeding season for the blue whales and their migration to a secret rendezvous somewhere in deep subtropical waters. During this period, the blue whales use the food stored in their blubber and eat very seldom as they pursue an age old ritual that enables the species to survive.

Blue whale survival as a species has been put in doubt by man's merciless pursuit. The huge leviathans surface every few minutes to exhale through the blow holes on top of their heads, spouting vapor high into the air, filling their lungs before submerging again. The cry of "Thar she blows," was shouted in some form or other for centuries, but for the great whales dwelling in the Antarctic, at home in the frigid southern reaches of the ocean, that cry was unheard until about the beginning of the twentieth century.

Whaling interests set up a whaling station on South Georgia Island, about a thousand miles east of the Falklands and north of the Orkney's. Ships used the station as a base and the cry of "Thar she blows" resounded across the frigid Antarctic waters followed by the echoing boom of the harpoon cannons. The killing irons with explosive heads fired from the bows of racing catcher boats much improved the whalers chances against the hapless creatures. The harpoon cannon had been perfected since its invention in 1860 by Sven Foyn in Norway.

Even the whaling station on South Georgia with its fleet of short-range catching boats was overshadowed by the advent of a new concept in whaling in 1925. For the first time, in the 1925–26 season, factory ships were introduced. These huge vessels with great mechanical winches and special slipways could haul aboard whole whale carcasses. Each factory ship had a fleet of iron, high-speed catcher boats and churned the Antarctic red with whale blood.

In the 1930–31 season, 41 factory ships plied the far reaches of the Antarctic waters with more than 200 catching boats between them. In that season alone 37,465 whales were taken. The toll of blue whales was 28,325. The incredible trauma inflicted on the whale population cannot be imagined. Whalers bragged of this world record catch until they found that their products were almost worthless, having flooded the market with whale goods.

Whaling continued with self-imposed industry quotas to keep the market price up until 1946, when representatives from countries taking part in the International Whaling Convention set up a commission to regulate whaling.

In an ill-advised act that spelled near total disaster for the world's last remaining blue whales, this International Whaling Commission established quotas in terms of Blue Whale Units (BWU). Since the blue whale is the largest of the whales, the commission's BWU meant it had targeted the most desirable catch. Each Blue Whale Unit was equal to 6 sei whales or 2 fin whales or 2½ humpbacks.

"Adoption of the Blue Whale Unit was the principal cause of the decline of the Antarctic whale resources," was the 1972 pronouncement of the International Whaling Commission, when they finally dropped the BWU system. This BWU concept was dropped after the estimated average 1933 to 1939 population of 33,000 blue whales was decimated to around 1000 to 3000 by 1963.

Even after the United Nations Conference on Human Environment recommended a complete ten-year moratorium on whales in 1972, the International Whaling Commission, with only four Japanese and three Russian expeditions working the 1971—72 Antarctic season, faced with a steady or complete decline in demand for baleen for use in corsets or whale oil for lamps and the wide preference for vegetable oils as a substitute for whale oil in food and cosmetics, banned the taking of blues and humpback whales, adopting for the first time in 1972 a species-by-species quota system.

The romantic notion of great sea leviathans cavorting in the ocean depths, making love, nursing their young with mammal milk, feeling and expressing strong filial and parental bonds, even communicating in a special language not fully understood by man, reserves a special place for whales in the natural scheme of things on Earth.

In 1979 at the International Whaling Conference meeting, all factory ship whaling was banned except for Antarctic minke whaling. The Indian Ocean north of 55° South was declared a whale sanctuary. In all of this negotiating, the United States representatives consistently took positions contrary to the recommendations of the conference's scientific committee. In setting the Iceland quotas for example, the United States urged a quota of 273 while the scientific committee recommended a quota of 103 whales. Either the scientific committee's judgment is wrong or the contrary American position is wrong. In either event, the world whale population is entirely too fragile to permit mistakes that will result in further depletion of these animal resources.

So little is known and so much is left to learn even about the mysteries of the sperm whales which migrate in exactly the opposite direction from the blues that care must be taken not to extinguish the entire species before man realizes their natural history. Researchers have followed the sperm whales southward from their normal habitats in warmer seas into the colder Antarctic each year. But still, science does not know whether there is some mysterious signal that causes the annual sperm whale migration or whether they are simply following the fish and giant squid, upon which they feed, south.

It may require decades for science to fully appreciate and understand the complex cycle of whale behavior. By the time we come to realize their importance in the cycle of nature, we may find that these endangered species are extinguished species.

SEA TURTLES

"There has not been an arribada of any size that I can remember in my lifetime. My father and grandfather spoke of them when I was a child," an elderly fisherman told me in Mexico. Yet they once came to the long white sand beaches in the Yucatan by the tens of thousands, great sea turtles: green turtles, ridleys and loggerheads. To make love in the warm Caribbean, then at evening, for the female to struggle ashore, moving her bulk over the wide stretch of beach to high ground to dig out a nest with her front flippers and deposit an even hundred fertilized eggs. With her labors done, the female would cover her nest and retreat to the sea, disappearing again for two to four years, until the cycle again somehow, mysteriously, repeats itself.

Sea turtles would return to their mating beaches in great arrivals or arribadas to repeat the mating-egg-laying cycle. Each time navigating hundreds or thousands of miles following some sense that has eluded the most careful detective work of scientists to understand. Following that mysterious sense, the sea turtles would return years later, at least seven or more years since birth until sexual maturity, to the exact beach where they were born.

Merciless turtle hunters would pounce on the gravid females as they arrived on their mating beaches, overturn them, and as the overturned turtles lay helplessly struggling, the hunters would cut off their bottom plate and extract thin strips of calipee. The calipee would later be dried and sold for use in making turtle soup. When their cruel work was done, the turtlers would leave the creatures suffering, entrails exposed, to be picked on by sea birds, eventually succumbing in the tropical sun.

What the turtle hunters did not kill, turtle-egg collectors did, digging up nests to gather the turtle eggs for sale. What the human egg collectors did not take, packs of wild dogs dug up and ate. The few hatchlings that survived steadily diminished until the great arribadas that once so grandly displayed the wonders of nature dwindled to the occasional arrivals of a few turtles to nest one or two at a time where they were born.

A friend of mine who has made a special study of sea turtles that regularly appear on the reefs off Palm Beach, Florida, has developed great personal insight into turtle behavior. Norine Rouse dives at least twice a day in the Gulf Stream off Florida's coast. Over the years she has been diving, she has noted the arrival each winter of a particularly large male turtle. There is no precise way to determine the turtle's age, but experts from the University of Florida suggest Norine's turtle

15

must be over 100 years old.

What was most surprising to Norine was that each summer the large male turtle would disappear only to return again to the same spot on the coral reef around December. The turtle became accustomed to divers from Norine's Diving Club of the Palm Beaches, and eventually they discovered that the turtle didn't like people riding on top of its shell, holding on behind the head. When Norine realized what was causing the turtle to steer away from human contact underwater, she stopped catching hold of the shell and instead would hold the turtle's front flipper. This the creature didn't seem to mind at all and once the understanding was reached, Norine and her students continued to cavort with their underwater friend.

Air breathing, sea turtles must swim to the surface for air but have great capacity for staying submerged on one breath for as much as a half-hour.

We had come back from a dive and were discussing some of Norine's observations on turtle behavior, when a former student called her with news that a sea turtle had become stranded on the

A stranded sea turtle is aided by diving instructor and naturalist, Norine Rouse. The plight of sea turtles has drawn international attention.

beach. We drove over to where the turtle had come ashore. There were no apparent signs usually associated with human cruelty. No gunshot wounds or harpoons. Unfortunately some people in boats often took to shooting turtles for fun as they surfaced for air. It was not immediately apparent to us or the Marine Patrol what caused the problem with this turtle. She was too weak to be put back to sea. The only visible signs of a potential problem were many barnacles attached to the shell and skin. If they were the boring kind, then their potential harm would occur as they drilled through the shell into the tissue.

As I watched Norine and the Florida Marine Patrol go to the aid of the stricken turtle, the impressive, rather heart-warming consequence of this experience was the concern expressed by the many people who stopped to watch. Ample numbers of young people offered assistance to lift the stricken animal, and a young man went home to borrow his father's truck to transport the turtle to an animal refuge for care. While our supposition was right, and the turtle finally died from the boring barnacles, the level of consciousness to the peril of these sea turtles has been raised. While this generation of North Americans may never see an arribada, perhaps it is not too optimistic to think that the sea turtle, like the whale, with appropriate surveillance and husbandry can be removed from the ever-growing list of endangered species.

2

Small and Beautiful Creatures

There are many small and unusual creatures in the sea. The curious diver could spend several hours observing their behavior patterns. Among the most interesting underwater phenomena are the ways creatures trap their food, move about, adopt disguises, reproduce, and relate to their environment. The serious diver, marine biology student, or behavioral scientist could be stimulated to develop fascinating and productive projects studying the way these ocean dwellers interact.

At first I didn't recognize the filamentous, white sticky material that adhered to my fins and wet suit. One can swim underwater observing creatures and never know how they feed or behave. Sticky filaments, like the ones that had adhered to me, are part of the feeding and defense mechanisms of sea cucumbers. These trepangs or *bêches de mer*, as they are called in Europe, dwell on the bottom. Some feed off sediment. Individual sea cucumbers may take from 100 to 300 pounds of bottom material into their systems each year. Some sea cucumbers trap their food in the sticky filaments, withdrawing them to digest the food.

Chemical substances which exude from the sea cucumbers' tough skin discourage predators. When threatened or squeezed by divers, the sea cucumber emits the filaments as a form of defense. Sea cucumbers are invertebrates, members of the echinoderm family.

They exist in a wide variety of shapes and colors. The bumps on the sea cucumbers skin contain nerve endings which give the animal a sense of feel. Some varieties of sea cucumber secrete holothurin, a substance that has medicinal value. While I cannot verify this from first hand experience, one of my French diving companions assures me that these *bêches de mer* are gustatory delights, quite edible if properly prepared.

Mollusks are among the most familiar of ocean life forms. Almost everyone who has strolled along a beach has stooped to pick up a sea shell.

Underwater, the observer's patience is rewarded with a fascinating variety of mollusks. There are more than 60,000 species of mollusks. Excluding insects, they are the most numerous animals existing on

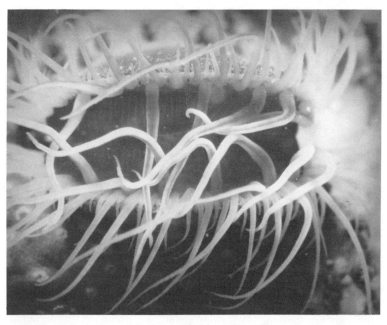

The lima clam is quite motile in the water, able to jump about and propel itself by opening and closing its shell. The filaments are extended for feeding.

Earth. Within the phylum Molluska are five classes. The Amphineura or chitons; Gastropoda (meaning stomach footed) or snails and snaillike shells; Schaphopoda, the tusk shells; Pelecypoda, the clams, mussels, scallops, and oysters; and the Cephalopoda or nautilus, squid, and octopus. The gastropods form the largest class of mollusks.

Gastropods include over 200 families or groups of shells, many among the most familiar species. They are called Gastropoda because of the "foot" that gives them locomotion in the water. Included in the gastropod class are the large shell families of limpets, top shells, turbine shells, horn shells, sea snails, sundials, conchs, cowries, helmet shells, tritons, whelks, olives, miters, cone shells, augers, and many more.

Guiding a group of divers in the Bahamas, I picked up a file shell or lima clam out of its niche in the rocks. As soon as my hand approached, this bivalve member of the pelecypod class of mollusks like clams and mussels, closed up. The delicate feeding tentacles withdrew and all that was left was a brown scallop shell. I set the file shell on a ledge and waited, signaling to the divers that they would see something special. We waited five minutes, still nothing. Waiting underwater somehow seems longer than waiting on land, but eventually our patience was rewarded. Slowly at first, the delicate feelers poked out of the shell. Then the shell opened wide, exposing a bright red mantle. Snapping its shell together, the file shell propelled itself through the water. The mollusk bounced and darted in front of us, seeking out a cranny where it would be protected from predators, yet still able to lure prey into its grasp. Once in a suitable crevice, the little mollusk is able to anchor itself by means of a small crochet at the base of the shell. There are a variety of free-swimming scallops that bound about, snapping their shells as a means of propulsion. The file shells are among the most beautiful because of their bright red and orange mantles.

Cowries are probably the most stunning of the gastropods. There are about 200 species of cowries. The French call these shells *porcelaines*. It is an apt description. Many cowries are more beautiful than the finest porcelain. When one considers the magnificence of even the simplest of these shells, it is readily apparent that they are truly a wonder of nature. One cowrie variety was so numerous in the South Pacific that they were once woven into chains and mats and used in barter as a form of currency. These small shells were named *moneta* or money cowries.

The living cowrie has a beautiful mantle which surrounds the shell. Extending up in two halves from the bottom, both halves meet at the top of the shell. The mantle forms and protects the shell from blemishes or encrusting organisms. When disturbed, the cowrie withdraws its mantle into the shell. Few people other than divers realize that the shell's mantle can be much more colorful and beautiful than the porcelain itself.

21

The flamingo tongue cowrie is a specialized shell that lives on soft coral. The flamingo browses on matter that settles on the coral, also devouring coral polyps. The flamingo's mantle is gaily bedecked with orange squares in beautiful patterns. The flamingo shell is an off-white pink. The shell, not nearly so beautiful as the living mantle is coveted by divers who wear them around their necks. In areas where the flamingo browses over the sediment on gorgonian coral, the over-harvesting of shells adversely affects the coral as well. It is sad to see barrels of flamingo shells for sale in curio shops, knowing the beauty they add to the reef environment.

Cone shells are among the most specially adapted of the gastropod mollusks. Some cone shells are able to shoot a poisoned dart to stun prey. Divers are taught to handle cone shells by the thick end and, as an extra precaution, to tap them with a snorkle before picking them up to insure that the dart mechanism is withdrawn into the shell.

Flamingo tongue cowrie. The bright orange squares are part of the mantle of the living shell.

One group of shell-less mollusks, among the most colorful creatures in the sea, are the nudibranchs. Nudibranchs, nudi meaning naked and branchia meaning gills, are actually mollusks without shells. Nudibranchs vary in size, some as tiny as 1/2 inch, others as large as 2 or 3 inches. These dragons of the sea browse along eating hydroids, immune from their stinging nematocysts. Novice divers, swimming 2 or 3 yards off the bottom, usually overlook these little creatures. Watching closely as the nudibranch undulates its body and inches along, tiny horns protruding from its head, delicate filamentous gills extending over the body, one can almost imagine these little creatures as dragons in miniature. The nudibranch is hemaphroditic, producing eggs and sperm in the same individual. When they mate, each individual exchanges sperm, fertilizing the other. A toxic substance secreted from a specialized gland makes the nudibranch quite unpalatable to predators which can quickly recognize and remember these brightly colored and untasty little creatures.

Puffer fish are unusual-looking creatures. Nonaggressive, slow swimmers, they are often set upon by divers who catch them by the tail, trapping them in their hands to make them puff up. Puffers fill their bodies with water, larger specimens attaining the size of a basketball. This natural defense mechanism makes them undelectable to predators. The puffer is equipped with spines that protrude when the fish is expanded. Bright green iridescent eyes give the fish an unusual appearance. Other varieties of puffers, found in parts of the Pacific and Indian Oceans are spotted in unusual patterns. These puffers swell up like their spiny cousins. The flesh and organs of puffer fish contain a poison. Fugu are relished in Japan, these puffers, however, must be prepared by specially licensed chefs who are trained to remove the poisons. The superstition that fugu acts as an aphrodisiac may account for the risks some Japanese are willing to take by consuming them.

By day they are balled up, seeking out crevices in basket sponges or niches in the reef. By night basket stars and marine crinoids or sea lilies, spread their arms to feed. Expanded, some basket stars may span 8 feet or more. Contracted, the animal would fit in the palm of one's hand. At the base, the crinoid has appendages that enable it to grip a piece of coral and move about. Crinoids are echinoderms, relatives of the starfish. They come in a variety of shapes and colors, often appearing in red and white or black and white patterns resembling feathers. Some crinoids appear in solid colors, those that are stark black are called widow crinoids. Diving at night, the underwater photographer has to be quick, for as soon as the dive light strikes the crinoid, the arms begin to fold up.

If a crinoid is removed from its hiding place during a daytime dive and held aloft by a diver, the arms begin to unfold and probe the water

The marine crinoid or sea lily is usually found with its arms folded during the day. At night the crinoid extends its arms to feed. Crinoids are marine animals, able to move about underwater.

entwining the diver's hand, looking for a substrate. As with puffer fish or any marine organism,if removed from their habitat for observation, the animal should be replaced so it can regain its home.

Sea anemone are coelenterates like the corals and jellyfish. Sea anemone are equipped with stinging cells which are used to paralyze food. They also provide a nasty sting if divers accidentally brush against them. Sea anemones are carnivorous, snatching hapless fish that meander within range of their tentacles. The anemone envelop the fish, drawing it toward the stoma or mouth in the center of the cavity. Certain damsel fish develop an immunity to the sting of the anemone's tentacles. These damsel fish, like the bright orange clown fish, live in a commensal relationship with the anemone. The clown fish lure other fish within range of the stinging tentacles. In turn, the little clown fish is afforded protection by the anemone, apparently developing a kind of chemical substance on their bodies that does not trigger the anemone's stinging cells. Tiny banded shrimp also inhabit sea anemone, seeking shelter and protection beneath the stinging cells.

Anemone add a flowerlike touch to shipwrecks and rocks in colder water. The anemone grow on stalks, long tentacles extended for feeding. Gardens of anemone can literally cover huge boulders underwater, their soft bodies and delicate structures adding color to the ecology.

I generally tell divers I take below for the first time on a tropical reef not to expect to see little square celluloid sponges growing on the rocks. Even so, I sometimes think people expect to see sponges growing in little rectangles of color, to be plucked from underwater trees, ready to go from harvest to kitchen sink. Either that, or novice divers have a notion that all sponges are yellow tan, round, and porous parazoan structures. This is the result of the image of Greek sponge divers bringing strings of commercial sponges to the surface. Sponges come in a variety of colors and unusual shapes, some with hard calcareous skeletons, some vaselike and soft.

Sponges, the simplest multicellular animals, belong to the family Porifera. While some species are dull in appearance, most varieties provide the bright color on a reef, stunningly bright oranges, pinks, reds, black, blue, purple, almost any color of the rainbow. Some sponges are flat, adapting to and growing over the substrate, some grow upright in tubular shapes resembling organ pipes, others look like baskets. Some sponges even resemble soft coral, their long tubular arms extending from a base, like branches of a tree.

Sponges feed by drawing water through their openings or external pores. The skeleton of the sponge is composed of calcarous or fibrous material. Food and oxygen are removed from the water that is drawn through the animal's pores. Using harmless dye, researchers have been able to observe water drawn into the sponge where it circulates in the internal cavity, then passing out through the oscule or central cavity. Sponges reproduce by budding or by external fertilization. Budding accounts for the colonial growth of sponges. Some sponges are free standing and have a hard body, like the basket sponges. Because of their shape and size, the French call this variety garbage-can sponges. To the touch, basket sponges are often mistaken for coral in hardness. Sponges have amazing regenerative power, able to replace damaged parts by new growth.

The big eye of the cuttlefish stares out from the night. Iridescent specks of green reflect back as the small creature seems to hover, mesmerized by the diver's light. The cuttlefish, a cephalopod mollusk, is related to the octopus and squid. It is considered by many a delicacy. The cuttlefish is capable of rapid color change by stimu-lating or relaxing muscles which are attached to chromatophores or small cells containing pigment. When the cells are stretched flat, the color is vivid; relaxed, the cell contracts so the color is not seen. The cuttlefish is equipped with a "cuttlebone"; using osmosis to absorb or expel water in this cuttlebone, the creature can control its buoyancy in the water.

The octopus is an exceptionally intelligent creature, capable of learning complicated behaviors. It is generally small, growing no more than a foot in total span. Larger varieties of the octopus are found in the cold Pacific coast off Washington and British Columbia. Even the large Pacific octopus, with three- or four-foot tentacles, has only a relatively small body. The octopus is a shy creature, generally hunting its food at night.

I was exploring an old cannon in the Mediterranean near a pier. Suddenly, picknickers dumped their trash into the water and an assortment of garbage tumbled down on top of me, including the end of a piece of salami. The salami fell in front of me near the cannon. In an instant, a cautious octopus poked its tentacles out of the cannon and grabbed the piece of salami, pulling it back into the cannon.

When I surfaced, one of the picknickers on the pier asked me what I saw. I told him I saw an octopus living in the cannon. The bather, apparently with a vested interest in food, now chewing on a piece of bread and cheese, asked me what an octopus eats. I was able to reply with some assurance that they eat salami.

The octopus uses its ability to camouflage itself by changing color to elude capture as well as a means of concealment enabling it to catch unwary fish. It is a predatory animal, seizing prey with its tentacles and holding it firm with two rows of suckers attached to each tentacle. The octopus has a sharp beak in the center of its body which it uses to devour its food. When disturbed by divers, the octopus tries first to get away, changes colors, then as a last resort, squirts a jet of ink and zips away at high speed with a motion of its tentacles and by blowing water through its siphon, expelling it in a jet.

The female octopus lays her eggs in strands in a protected part of the reef. She will defend these eggs for four months, cleaning them with suckers on the underside of her tentacles. Only a few of the hundred thousand eggs survive to maturity, most fall prey to hungry fish as soon as they are hatched.

Jellyfish, long the bane of swimmers, are among the most beautiful animals to observe underwater. Coelenterates, these medusae propel themselves through the water, delicately undulating their bodies, trailing stinging tentacles behind. The Portuguese man-of-war may draw its stinging tentacles 15 or more feet behind or under its body. In some cases, where there is an allergic reaction, the sting of the jellyfish can be fatal to humans. Portugese man-of-war jellyfish float on the surface of the water by inflating a purple sack with gas.

A friend of mine was conditioning himself by swimming far offshore with mask, fins and snorkle in Martinique in the French West Indies. Without seeing them until it was too late, my friend swam into a mass of jellyfish. He received multiple stings on the face and chest. By the time he managed to swim ashore, the stings had swollen and he was developing the symptoms of shock. His breath was short, coming in gasps. In addition to the painfall stings, he complained of pains in his chest. Our diving doctor immediately administered antihistamines and spread cortisone cream on the stings. Shortly thereafter, the pain subsided and breathing returned to normal. As a result of this experience, my friend vowed never to swim or dive without the protection of a wet suit. Had it not been for the quick work of our experienced diving physician, my friend's encounter with the jellyfish could have had far more serious consequences.

Starfish are interesting creatures. Their shapes and sizes are as

The Crown of Thorns starfish has long been considered the scourge of coral reefs, grazing over coral and killing large segments of the reef. The picture shows the underside of the starfish. It is best not to touch or handle the Crown of Thorns, Acanthaster planci, *with bare hands, as the sharp spines contain a venom that can cause a painful wound.*

varied as their shades of color. Starfish, members of the echinoderm phylum, feed on mussels or other mollusks. The starfish grasps the mussel with suckers on its arms and applies steady pressure until the shell can no longer resist. With the shell open, the starfish extends its stomach and externally digests its meal.

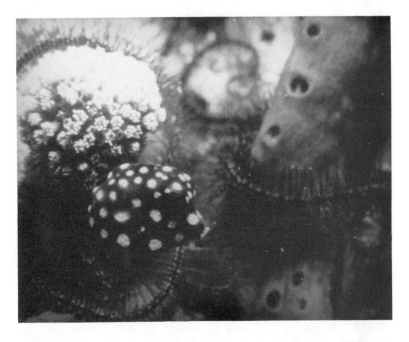

Juvenile creatures of the reef often resemble their parents in miniature. This baby box fish concealed itself among coral growth for protection. It is shown here in a macro close-up photograph. The fish is actually only the size of a small fingernail.

I spent nearly a whole dive watching a juvenile box fish. The small spotted creature would duck into niches in the coral, its tiny fins fanning furiously, giving the little fish a helicopter effect. Finally, just as my patience was almost exhausted, the little fish popped out of the coral and I was able to snap its picture. The fish was about as big as the tip of a finger, sporting yellow polka dots. Adult box fish or trunk fish as they are sometimes called, have hard triangular-shaped bodies. They are a slow-moving fish and interesting to observe. Prized for soup in the West Indies, fishermen prepare a delicious bouillabaise with them.

The trumpet fish camouflages itself by freezing in the vertical next to a piece of soft coral or sponge. It is an amazing form of adaptive behavior, as instinctive in the juvenile as in the adult. Swimming around branches of gorgonian coral, the alert diver will usually spot these trumpet fish only by looking carefully to distinguish them from branches of coral.

One of the most interesting fish to observe underwater is the parrot fish. By day these fish are seen biting off chunks of the coral with their beaks. The parrot fish eat the algae in the coral and discharge undigested matter as sand. One of the parrot fish defense mechanisms is to defecate on the approach of anything they deem threatening. The theory apparently is that the predator may be confused or stop to investigate the fecal discharge as the parrot fish swims off.

The constant nibbling at the coral produces a significant formation of coral sand, eventually adding to beach deposits. At night, the parrot fish secretes a cocoon of mucus from its skin. The first time I saw this phenomenon on a night dive, I was fascinated by the fish in the bubble. The mucus enveloped the entire fish in a clear plastic balloon as the fish slept in a crevice under a rock. Researchers theorize that this mucus bubble protects the parrot fish while it sleeps, blocking out the scent which would attract predators. The horny beak of the parrot fish is specially adapted to its coral eating habits.

"What on Earth was it?" one of the divers exclaimed when we surfaced from a shallow dive in the Bahamas. "Bat fish," I replied, wiping the water out of my eyes. All of us were particularly proud of the photos we had taken of this curious specimen. Its body shape resembles a kind of glider; its skin knurled and knobby. Actually the fish, generally not more than a foot long, depends on its mottled appearance as a form of camouflage. The bat fish remains sedentary on the bottom, luring fish that happen into its presence by jiggling a little appendage from its face. The fish has aileronlike feet that enable it to walk on the bottom. In spite of its ungainly appearance, the bat fish is capable of short bursts of speed, propelled by a swish of its tail when required to catch prey. The bat fish is a harmless bottom dweller, interesting to observe underwater, quite photogenic, its shape and appearance resembling something from another planet.

Many tropical reef fish have garish designs and blaring stripes. Over time these adaptations have created a benefit, enabling the fish to evade predation. Many of the groupers or sea bass are beautifully colored in violets, browns, and grays. Some varieties sport speckled patterns and patches that help camouflage the fish among the coral. The grouper is often seen lounging in the doorway of its cave or nook

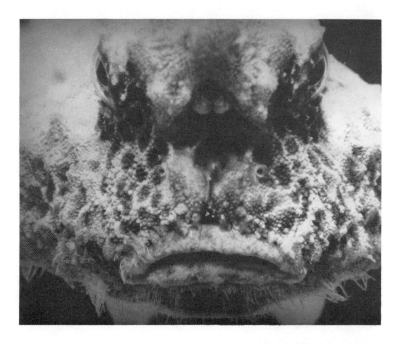

A bat fish, lies placidly on the bottom, waiting for prey to come within range. (Bahamas)

in the coral. When the grouper sees a tasty fish happen by, it opens its large mouth and creates a vacuum effect using its gills, sucking the prey down with a gulp.

One of the most beautiful of the groupers is the emperor sea bass, *Variola iouti*. This scarlet fish with a variety of violet speckles, is one of the most colorful in the sea. *Variola* is common in the South Pacific and provides divers with a shocking rainbow of reds and purple, aptly deserving the designation emperor.

Little pedestrian blennies and gobies are curious rascals. They manage to turn up in the oddest places. I've seen these perennial reef fish poking their heads out of the neck of disgarded bottles, in holes burrowed in pieces of coral or ensconced in pieces of sponge. At the approach of a diver, the blenny will retreat into the secure confines of its little home. Too curious to remain concealed long, the little blenny will reward the patient diver by poking its head out of the coral. Eyes rotating, the blenny seems to be looking in all directions at once.

Tube worms, Christmas tree worms, and feather dusters construct their homes on a substrate of coral. These creatures secrete a tubular home with only a tiny opening exposed. The plume worms protect the entrance to their homes with a sharp spike. Christmas tree worms or plume worms are members of the serpulid family. They are brightly colored and secrete a hard limestone home. Like the plume worms, the feather duster or sabellid worms extend their feathery gills from their homes to breathe. These animals feed by filtering the water for small food particles. At the approach of a diver, the Christmas tree worms and feather dusters draw back quickly into their tubular homes. It requires patience and skill to take close-up photographs of these colorful tube worms underwater.

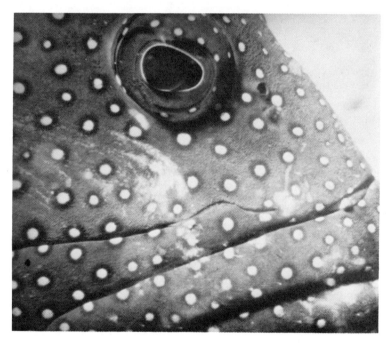

The grouper is one of the hunters of the reef. If undisturbed, some species can grow to weigh several hundred pounds. Grouper are usually territorial fish, found in their usual caves or rocky crevices dive after dive.

The little seahorse is a rare treat for underwater photographers. The female seahorse deposits her eggs in the male's pouch where they are fertilized and incubated for as many as 10 days. The male seahorse gives birth to live baby miniatures by contracting and expanding its body in jerking motions. Seahorses have a dorsal fin that enables them

Christmas tree worms or plume worms, Spirobranchus giganteus, *are relatives of terrestrial worms. Like the feather dusters, they extend their delicate spirals to feed. At the slightest disturbance, the plumes retract, revealing a sharp thornlike protrusion on the face of the coral that can inflict a nasty cut.*

to swim underwater. They are ungainly swimmers, preferring to wrap their tails around an object underwater remaining out of the current. Horny projections and camouflage patterns aid the seahorse in escaping predation. It requires a keen eye underwater to discover these little creatures.

Crustaceans are most often seen served with parsley and drawn butter. Underwater, shrimp and lobster are an important part of the reef life. Commercially, it requires about seven years for a cold water lobster to grow to legal size, weighing about 1 pound and measuring 3 3/16 inches from eye socket to the end of the carapace. Many dive clubs in New England, New York, and New Jersey make ritual trips to shipwrecks or rocky reaches in the Atlantic to catch lobster for a summer beach barbeque. The large crusher and holding claw are absent in the spiny rock lobster or langouste, tropical water cousin of the northern lobster. Lobster are noisy underwater, their crackling noises are heard throughout the reef as they rattle in their caves and nitches under coral heads.

I watched over a period of months while divers constructed an aquarium 10 feet from a Polynesian lagoon. They thought the aquarium would be interesting to hotel guests. Each time they added fish, the fish would die, until the inexperienced aquarium builders determined the necessary balance of coral and reef life. When the aquarium was finished the hapless fish swam back and forth in their glass cage. Only a couple of steps away in the shallow lagoon, a snorkler or anyone so inclined to sit in the hotel's glass bottomed boat, could observe these same marine creatures in their own environment. The aquarium was an object lesson. To understand and appreciate the wonder of life in the sea, to enjoy and understand the relationships of these small and beautiful creatures of the deep, one must undertake a partnership with the underwater environment. A gentle intrusion is all that is required to enjoy the beauty of the smaller creatures in the ocean realm.

3

Coral, the Mighty Builders

It is everywhere. Coral—the pervasive topography of any tropical reef—is actually many diverse species of marine animals that begin life as free swimming larvae and end up the foundation of undersea nations. Even the name conjures up mental images of atolls and fringing reefs, of tropical sand beaches, and fine jewelry more precious than gold.

Coral was recognized by early Chinese and Egyptian cultures, chronicled and coveted in Biblical times. It wasn't until the eighteenth century when Jean-Andre Peysonnel observed coral feeding on zooplankton and reported the carnivorous habits of coral polyps that science came to a modern understanding of these colonial animals.

Coral requires warm clear water with ample sunlight in order to flourish. Ideal coral growth conditions include a water temperature that never falls below 68°F. The clarity of the water enables the sunlight to penetrate, thus making it rare to find coral growth at depths in excess of 200 feet, with notable exceptions in particularly clear water.

Recent studies have shown that algae living inside coral polyps bear an important relationship to coral growth. These algae, called zooxanthellae, use the carbon dioxide produced as a waste product by exhalations of the coral animal host. The carbon dioxide is converted into starch by the algae. During the process of conversion, the zooxanthellae use sulphur, nitrogen, and phosphorous, elements also excreted during the coral polyp's metabolic processes. By using coral wastes, the algae eliminate the need for the polyps to expel them. In this way, the zooxanthellae increase the coral's efficiency, saving the animal energy which it uses instead in the construction of a limestone theca or skeleton.

Like all plants, zooxanthellae require light. The more light there is, the better the efficiency of these algae. In the absence of light they die. Zooxanthellae produce oxygen, but the extent to which oxygen produced by algae assist coral growth is not completely known.

An experiment was conducted to determine the relationship between coral growth and the algae living inside the polyps. Coral was placed in a box without light. When the algae died from lack of light, the coral continued to live, but their growth rate decreased markedly. It was found that the coral grew ten times faster in light with zooxanthellae, than it did in the dark without the algae. A clear indication of the important but little understood relationships between these minute plants and coral in the marine environment.

Zooxanthellae themselves are small brown algae only about one-hundredth of a millimeter in diameter. In tiny coral larvae, not more than 1 millimeter in length, researchers counted 7400 of these small zooxanthellae. While all of the intricate biological relationships are not yet fully understood, it is clear that each of these living things derive mutual benefit from the other and have, over time, found harmonious living relationships beneficial.

It was only in the 1960s that the relationship between coral growth and zooxanthellae was understood. The lack of abundant coral growth at extreme depths and the flourishing coral gardens near the surface where there is ample light penetration, is explained by the presence of these minute plants.

Some forms of hard, dense coral grow at extreme depths. The Mediterranean coral diver plies his trade, seeking valuable branches of red coral in the only area of the world where this gem quality coral is found, deep inside caverns and nitches, almost completely sheltered from sunlight. It has been said that this variety of dense red coral grows only 1 centimeter in every hundred years.

Hard rose coral has been found by divers using submersible recovery vehicles in the great depths of the Pacific off Hawaii's coast. Mechanical arms harvest this variety of deep ocean coral dropping it in wire mesh baskets. Gem cutters on Oahu cut and polish them into fine jewelry.

Coral reproduces in two distinct ways. Coral polyps release sperm into the water which fertilize eggs inside other polyps. This sexual fertilization results in the development of larvae or planulae. As the planulae mature, they leave the polyp as bulblike organisms with microscopic hairs which undulate, keeping the larvae afloat on the surface. These larvae feed and drift until eventually settling on a hard surface where they attach and begin to develop. Thereafter, the coral polyp reproduces asexually by budding. A polyp splits off from the first, developing an identical but separate adult structure. This budding continues, and, before long, a colony develops in geometric proportions.

CORAL GROWTH

Relatively little is known about coral growth. While diving with the National Geographic Society team on Truk in Micronesia, I observed the importance of having a substrate of known origin. Coral was measured and tagged with metal tags. We could assume that the growth over the shipwrecks had taken place in the more than thirty-five years since their sinking. When these same coral heads and branches are measured again, science will have a better idea of the yearly growth rate of coral over a period where water, air, and climactic conditions have been monitored.

Present studies show generally that acropora or staghorn coral grows at the rate of about 2 inches a year while the dense, round mass of brain coral increases in yearly overall growth only about 1/15 of an inch.

By examining coral growth, scientists can determine periods of hard times or turmoil on Earth. Study of coral growth helped researchers determine the collapse of the Earth's reef community at least two, perhaps four or more times over history. With each collapse, the entire face of the Earth changed, and with it whole species of beings became extinct.

The first major reef collapse occurred 500 to 600 million years ago. The last collapse of the reef communities occurred as best as can be determined, some 65 million years ago. This last collapse marked the end of the Cretaceous period when 2/3 of the coral families and 1/3 of the animal families became extinct. This marked the end of the dinosaur, the upwelling of the Earth's cores and the creation of basins in the sea. These basins changed the complexion of the Earth's form.

Water that once covered most of what we know today as great land masses was drained off into these basins leaving vast areas that were submerged, high and dry.

In the Cenozoic era the polar ice caps were formed creating radical changes in the Earth's temperature, some 20 million years ago. Ocean currents changed and the cold water killed off coral, driving the marine animals into what are now tropical oceans. The coral reefs established themselves and built upon rock upwellings, obstructions and dead limestone skeletons of their fellows, forming massive barriers, atolls, and fringing reefs we know today.

Researchers have developed new techniques using X-rays to study coral growth. While there are only a handful of scientists in the world pursuing this important area of study, great progress has been made in analyzing coral growth from X-ray photographs.

Geologists learned of the great turmoils on the face of the Earth, periods of ample and prolific growth, by analyzing these growth rings and patterns left by coral skeletons. The principal of studying coral growth rings is similar to the way growth rings of trees are studied.

The collected coral is sliced to about 1/2 centimeter, then placed on top of Kodak Industrex AA X-ray film. With a setting of 100 kV the coral is exposed for 10 to 60 seconds, the X-ray source being about 50 inches distant from the film. The X-ray negative is then processed to make a positive or print. The resultant picture is used as a map to study the coral growth.

When coral growth rates are correlated to other geological information, important extrapolations can be made about nutrient supply and climatic conditions, and rather sophisticated ecological and biological theories can be tested or supported by the findings.

Recent studies in Bermuda have shown the effects of dredging on coral growth. It has been supposed for years that silting over and its effect on water clarity due to dredging have profound negative results on the entire underwater reef system. This was confirmed in the Bermuda studies, using the coral radiographs taken from Castle Harbor. The coral died between 1941 and 1943, when dredging was done to deepen the port.

Flying over the French Society Islands in Polynesia, the stunning beauty of coral waters and fringing reefs gives majestic testimony to the work of these tiny coral polyps, some individuals not even so large around as a pencil point. Walking on the jagged surface of these reefs gives another impression altogether. Looking closely, one is quick to observe the complex interaction of plants and animals living together on the reef.

In examining the ecological relationships of coral, researchers believe that the solubility of calcium carbonate in warm water accounts for the tropical range of corals. The limestone skeletons of coral are made up principally of calcium carbonate which is present, dissolved in sea water. It is easier for organisms to extract calcium from sea water in warmer temperatures than cold.

Coral growth near land masses occurs generally as atolls, fringing reefs, or barrier reefs. An atoll is what one classically visualizes when calling up a mental image of a coral island reef. Atolls are ringlike islands surrounding a lagoon with passes through to the ocean.

Charles Darwin was one of the first to propose a theory of how coral atolls originated. He began his observations in 1836, toward the end of the historic voyage of *The Beagle*. Darwin originated the theory that atolls grew up as the islands themselves sank into the sea. Darwin's early studies have been confirmed by deep borings and core samples from the reefs.

Studying coral growth, Darwin theorized that atolls began as fringing reefs on islands subsiding into the ocean. The coral kept growing upward toward the surface as the island slowly sank into the ocean. When the island itself disappeared, the hard coral reefs were left.

When scientists bored into Eniwetok Island in the Pacific, coral was found in core samples taken as deep as 4000 feet. At that level no more coral was found, and the drills hit basalt foundation material. The only logical explanation for finding coral at 4000 feet in the middle of the Pacific is that a great sea mount or island gradually, over time, subsided into the sea, much as Darwin first theorized.

Oddly enough, coral has been found high and dry on the peaks of mountains, far from the present borders of the ocean. These coral formations have been nicknamed "atolls on mountains." Geologists who discovered these massive coral formations on the Malay Archipelago at an altitude of 4,000 feet above sea level were forced to conclude that while parts of the Earth must have subsided into the sea, other parts must have been elevated.

Without naming it, Darwin's early studies of coral reefs gave rise to the concept of the Earth's equilibrium. Isostasy or isostastic theories hold that the Earth seeks constant equilibrium around its core. Considerable weight change in one area results in changing weight in another until equilibrium is attained. While only theoretical, this seeking equilibrium may account for earthquakes and great under-ocean land slides, upwellings and tumults in the Earth's crust. The theory is quite simple. It appears geologically as well as in the animate world of creatures—nature seeks balance and equilibrium. A balance that is often quite delicate.

ULTIMATE CORAL VIEWING

One of the largest atolls in the world is the South Pacific Tuamotu Island of Rangiroa. The lagoon in Rangiroa stretches some 70 kilometers long and is about 30 kilometers wide. Since the geography in Rangiroa is so extreme, large areas of the reef have never been explored. On the larger wider areas of the atoll, settlements have sprung up, although even at its widest point it requires only a minute to walk from lagoon to ocean.

From the air, Rangiroa displays one of the most beautiful panoramas in the world, turquoise and opaline water on the lagoon side where the shallow sandy bottom reflects the sunlight, dark blue on the ocean side, where the depths drop off rapidly to more than five thousand feet a short distance from shore.

Fringing reefs are simply coral formations that grow out along the shore of islands or land masses. One of the most beautiful examples of a fringing reef is found in the water surrounding the island of Martinique in the French West Indies. Rocky areas underwater have provided the substrate for attaching coral organisms, and around these rocky outcroppings magnificent coral gardens of great variety and color flourish.

Offshore rock islands in Martinique, such as Le Diamant on the South and La Perle in the North, provide some of the best diving in the world for those interested in studying coral growth. Brightly colored gorgonians abound among the natural underwater cliffs and rocky archways. The gradually sloping reefs which grow away from these islands into the sea provide ideal conditions for hard coral growth. Martinique's reefs of coral are sculptured underwater flower gardens in a crystal bowl.

Reefs that grow up offshore appearing as distant breakwaters with channels between the reef itself and the land mass are called barrier reefs. The Great Barrier reef along Australia's North Coast stretches for 1260 miles, covering an area of some 100,000 square miles. Australia's Barrier Reef lies between 10 and 100 miles offshore from the main Australian coast. It is amazing, when one considers that these great coral reefs were constructed by small polyps, not even 1/2 inch long.

CORAL BIOLOGY AND ECOLOGY

Among the most beautiful corals are the sea fans, sea feathers and sea whips. Some mistakenly identify these soft corals as plants. They are sometimes referred to as false corals or octocorals.

Soft, fanlike octocorals are called gorgonians, named for the wild-haired sisters of Greek mythology whose stare turned men to stone. Like true hard corals, Gorgonia are colonial animals with interconnected polyps. Gorgonians secrete calcareous material, attach themselves to rock or other suitable substrate and reproduce by asexual budding as well as by fertilization.

The octocorals provide some of the most vibrant color to a reef, growing in bright purples, reds, oranges, and yellows. Some gorgonian coral have a pharmaceutical use in making prostaglandins, a birth

Divers in the tropics are warned to "look, but don't touch." Touching a piece of fire coral like this will result in hundreds of nematocysts, the hairlike protrusions in the photograph, being discharged into the skin. The affected area will redden and pain and discomfort may persist for many days.

control pill.

Coral species have adapted to a variety of life styles. Their exotic

41

shapes often determine the names given them, such as elkhorn coral or staghorn coral or brain coral.

In varying degrees, coral polyps are equipped with stinging cells. While most varieties are innocuous to man, the nematocysts of fire coral, the mustard-colored cactus of the undersea, can provide nasty stings, often accompanied by an allergic reaction that may last for several days.

Understanding the relationships between coral growth and the reef environment is giving science a new awareness of the fragile ecological balance underwater. Dredging and construction along Florida's coastlines like the excessive building, population pressure, and dredging in Tahiti have taken vast tolls in terms of destroying important natural resources.

Over a protracted period of study, I was able to track the silting over of coral reefs inside Moorea's lagoon in Tahiti. Part of the problem was caused by construction and run off from the land. Some of the damage was caused by the dumping of excavated material into the water to form artificial Tuamotus or jettylike protrusions out from shore into the lagoon.

Over one particularly beautiful shallow coral reef near one of these artificial jetties, most of the coral was dead. Heavy silt blanketed the coral and much of the base of the reef was submerged in silt and sand. This reef was a shell collector's favorite, so there was a great deal of physical breakage by snorklers using iron bars to get at the shells.

The clarity of the lagoon was generally affected by the dumping and construction. Toilet and kitchen waste was being pumped into the lagoon in quantities never before known in the area. Waste matter was increased due to the massive influx of tourism. This waste added to the decreased clarity of the water. Lack of clarity will have long-term effects on the reef environment and eventually suppress coral growth inside the lagoon. Silting over, however, was having and will have immediate, dramatic results. Huge masses of the reef were dead or dying. Silt was being carried out through the passes and had begun to affect the coral on the ocean side of the reef.

Although I made several inquiries as to why officials were dumping dirt and excavated rock into Moorea's lagoon to form these artificial Tuamotus, which in the overall complexion of the area added nothing to nature's majesty, I was unable to obtain a satisfactory answer. One response that more or less accounted for the truth had something to do with the desire to employ people on the project, to build what they thought would be aesthetic artificial jetties near influential persons' land, and to provide a convenient dump site for excavated earth.

Whatever the reason, this attempt to adjust nature to suit man's needs or desires was having profound detrimental effects on the underwater environment.

A friend of mine continually talks about "people pollution." While I often dismiss this observation as grousing, it was evident from the flocculent material floating on the surface of Moorea's lagoon and the suspended kitchen dumpings, detergent, and toilet waste in the shallow water that massive doses of visitors with their resultant generation of waste was more than the environment could support over an extended period.

Outside the lagoon I observed the incursion of *Acathanster planci*, the notorious coral-eating Crown of Thorns starfish. This browsing, predatory echinoderm was well established on the ocean reefs. Many of the madrepore, free-standing, small, hard coral, dislike in shape, had already been decimated by the Crown of Thorns, and the voracious creatures were impacting a variety of coral species on the reef.

While more recent theories consider incursions by the Crown of Thorns starfish cyclical and part of the balancing process of nature, others still give some credence to the theory that where the triton sea snail exists in large numbers the large mollusk acts to control the starfish.

I attempted to study the relationship between the triton and the Crown of Thorns in Tahiti in a controlled environment. Having captured healthy specimens on the ocean reef, we placed them together in a series of different ways in the shallower water of the lagoon where they could be observed.

The tactile reaction of the triton was observed several times in each series as it came upon or in contact with the Crown of Thorns. This contact was created by having divers place the triton in contact with the starfish or waiting patiently on the mini-reef for natural encounters. It appeared that the giant sea snails were essentially disinterested in the starfish (in Polynesia at least), preferring other diets and probably not effecting any significant control whatsoever of the Crown of Thorns.

In many months of diving, I was unable to observe any predation by the wild triton on the starfish in the natural ocean environment. While wild populations of the snail were decreased by shell collectors, even on remote sections of the Tahitian reefs, inaccessible to shell hunters, there was inconclusive evidence to support any theory that the Triton sea snail was an effective natural enemy of the coral eating Crown of Thorns.

In Florida, off Riviera Beach, along the Intra-Coastal Waterway, divers had constructed a series of artificial reefs. While these reefs attracted a wide variety of reef builder organisms and fish, the divers were able to observe the growth decrease as the area silted over. The principal cause of this silting was dredging and construction of a large bridge connecting the causeway on West Palm Beach with Palm Beach Shores, about 1 mile North of the artificial underwater reef site.

The effect of silting on water clarity and coral growth is dramatic. In a relatively short time, ill-conceived progress can destroy what it has taken nature eons to create. While no one yet knows the total effect careless depletion of a reef environment will have over a long period, the short-term effects will be to cut off one of the main reasons tourists visit these tropical areas, making for the construction boom in the first place—the natural beauty of the environment.

Acting as an underwater instructor in the Mediterranean, along one of the few remaining coastal regions in Spain where heavy industry and pollution had not taken a severe toll on the reef ecology, I was astounded by the reckless, selfish foraging of divers seeking out branches of red coral. Even in the remote, seemingly inaccessible reaches of this Spanish coast, one would have to dive to depths exceeding 50 meters to see red coral of any appreciable size, due to the pressure of coral collectors seeking out this valuable resource.

On one occasion, while guiding a group of divers, I observed a man hammering away at small branches of red coral, destroying an entire area of the reef with his large hammer. The man came away with a tiny branchlet not more than 2 centimeters long. While it is difficult to account for this kind of irresponsible destruction by divers who should appreciate the beauty of a reef environment, it is really not much different from the irresponsible commerce in coral. Many persons have seen the sad spectacle, tons of coral piled in heaps, bleached out in the sun along tourist highways like U.S. 1 in South Florida's Keys, or what is seen in rows at the street markets of Maui or Oahu in Hawaii.

Man has taken coral from the sea often to the point of depletion, without realizing that its sale dead decreases the value of the land by programming aesthetic destruction of the reef. This is not to say that within limits nature cannot be replenished by new growth. It is quite sad, however, to be witness to the wholesale and utter destruction to vast underwater areas by greed, overharvesting, reckless abuse, and of course, one of the most radical offenders, industrial pollution.

The importance of water clarity for coral growth is evident by the study of the way reefs grow in nature. Where fresh, clear ocean water washes over a reef, the coral growth is more prolific than on the lee side of the same reef where dirt and sand are deposited. Fringing reefs grow out to sea, responding to the more favorable conditions to windward. These environmental conditions must be preserved if the coral reefs are to survive.

The beauty of a coral reef and the complex interdependence of life are evident to any diver whose angle of vision is first wide, then narrow. Looking closely on a reef opens horizons not readily apparent superficially. An experienced diver can find interest, spending long periods of time underwater without covering great distances. While reefs can be massive, stretching for miles underwater, it is only by looking closely that one comes to appreciate the fragile and delicate relationships between plants and animals. By looking closely, the individual coral polyp stands out as a mightly toiler in the sea, one tiny builder of only one tiny section of a great underwater pyramid of life.

"Travellers tell us of the vast dimensions of the pyramids and other great ruins," Darwin wrote in his Journal. He then went on to describe his observations of coral reefs, commenting, "but utterly insignificant are the greatest of these (ruins) when compared to these underwater mountains of stone."

4

Hide and Seek on the Ocean Floor

Having an edge in nature means survival. Things evolve. If they survive, if they are able to reproduce, and if their offspring survive, then the species continues. Biology usually follows a regular pattern wherein ontogeny recapitulates phylogeny, or like begets like. However, over the course of thousands or millions of replications, statistically, traits will develop in some of the individuals that set them apart. Albinos are born, eccentric colors develop, variances that are seemingly oddities when compared with the population are noticed. Scientists refer to some of these hereditary oddities as mutations.

If the mutation or eccentric trait is beneficial, then the mutant survives. If the trait is a burden, then often the oddity is selected out in the natural process. If the trait neither provides a benefit nor a burden, then like as not it will continue, relatively unnoticed in the general population. Not every beneficial trait survives. Accidents may cause the better-adapted variety to be killed instead of the less well adapted, leaving much to chance in the species' survival.

Where a trait develops and it gives an organism an edge, a benefit over others in the general population, then, over time, the members of the species with this beneficial trait will survive to reproduce in greater numbers than the template or original variety. The beneficial trait is passed along to successive generations, eventually the entire popu-

47

lation of the species. Where a new species is thus created, this is called speciation. Speciation is not something that occurs overnight, or even over several years. The development and evolution of such a trait may require many generations before it is even observed in the population and many thousands of generations before the beneficial trait becomes the norm. The trait develops because it enables the organism to better cope in its environment.

The development of these special characteristics that enable organisms to survive in their environment is called adaptation. The word is used in two senses: adaptation per se, meaning alterations in the species wherein organisms possess particular characteristics enabling them to survive in their environment, and adaptive behavior which refers to physiological adjustments that enable organisms to cope with fluctuations in their immediate environment. This adaptive behavior or the adjustments themselves are also called adaptations, but used this way the word relates to the flexibility of the organism to change or adapt to its changing environment rather than the process of altering the species through evolution.

In nature, there is very little that is without purpose. It may not always be apparent to the observer, and it may be difficult to determine why something evolved the way it did. The reason for a particular adaptation may have long ago disappeared, while the trait remained as a vestige in the creature's genetic memory. Even lurid colors play a specific role in nature. A species that fails to adapt to its environment may exist temporarily, but it is doomed to eventual extinction.

Animals and plants exist in nature because they are able to cope in their environment. Their species characteristics enable them to survive in the conditions of life surrounding them. If a species is in discord or disharmony with its environment and cannot adapt to it, the species will die out. If an individual organism within the species does not possess the species' adaptive qualities, the individual dies out. If the environment changes and the organism does not possess flexibility to adapt, behaviorally or physiologically, to the new situation, then it will die out.

Simplistically, a seal, to exist in the sea developed flippers. A seal without flippers could not exist in its marine environment. Seals whose flippers are particularly affected by pollution in their environment, and thus develop disease, will die out as their environment becomes polluted.

Man, although sophisticated and societal and able to adapt to a wide range of environments, is totally dependent on his environment and the natural balance. Although we have tried to adjust nature to suit man's convenience, we have seen all too often that we have failed massively. How creatures survive in the seas and oceans, how their particular adaptive traits enable them to cope with their environment and thus live to produce surviving offspring takes many miraculous forms. To the human observer, natural camouflage, protective coloration, mimicry, highly specialized poison, defensive mechanisms, and cryptic behavior patterns may seem curious and unusual. To the creature itself, it is a means of survival, an adaptation that enables it to cope in their habitat.

I examined the slide several times. It appeared to have been properly exposed, but I could see nothing on it. Before throwing it out, I went to my notes to see why there was nothing on my picture. After reading my notes, I looked again. Once I knew it was there, the outline was unmistakable. Lying perfectly still in the sand, the flatfish can elude even the eye of a carefully trained observer. The fish was perfectly camouflaged in the sand, matching the color and pattern.

Many marine creatures possess the ability to change color underwater, to blend in with their surroundings. Color change may also reflect anger, courtship, or simply the animal's mood. Color change may be used to warn, lure, attract, dissuade, hide, or repel, and may be achieved in a number of ways.

At first scientists classified imitation or mimicry by whether the mimic imitated objects, as in the case of the flatfish imitating the color of sand. This was called mimesis. If the imitated object was of plant origin then it was called phytomimesis; of animal origin, zoomimesis. Confusion in classifying the objects mimed led to the abandonment of this terminology and now mimicry is generally classified by whether the signal is of interest to the signal-receiver imitated. If so, then this is mimicry. If the background or substrate is imitated, then it is termed camouflage or mimesis.

In the flounderlike windowpane fish (*Scophthalmus aquosus*) or peacock flounder (*Bothus lunatus*), thousands of cells, called chromatophores are contained in the skin. Each of these cells or chromatophores contains a pigment. They may be red, orange, yellow, green, blue, silver, black, or brown. By expanding or contracting these chromatophores, the fish can change its color to match the bottom on which it rests.

Experiments have been conducted with these flatfish by placing them in different colored tanks. Placed in a light tank, the fish appeared white. Moved into a tank with a dark bottom, the fish expanded its dark color cells and became dark. When the fish was placed over a checkerboard surface, it expanded black and red cells to

49

match.

Scientists then blindfolded the fish and found that it failed to alter color. This proved that the fish's eyes tell it what pattern to copy.

In the South Pacific, I observed a peacock flounder lying camouflaged in the sand. I disturbed it from its resting place, following it underwater until the flatfish lighted on the wreck of an old ship. In a few seconds, the flounder had expanded its dark cells to match the rusted iron ship's plate. When I disturbed the fish again, it swam over a section of the reef and almost immediately altered color to match its new surroundings.

In varying degrees, most flatfish are able to change their color. The Atlantic winter flounder often elude detection, lying so placidly and perfectly camouflaged in the sand, that one almost has to discern the eyes to know it's a fish. Flatfish also possess a number of false eye spots on their dorsal surface as an added disguise to elude enemies. This camouflage is not uniquely defensive. Lying disguised on the bottom, the flatfish can simply wait for dinner to pass by, then snap it up.

Diving in Florida, at slack tide in the Palm Beach Inlet, I observed a regular quick change artist at work. A small triggerfish was curious about what I was doing, diving around its nest. He posed for a picture, then darted a short distance away. As the background changed so did the fish's color. It developed a mottled dark-and-whitish pattern. I exposed a few frames in succession as the little critter changed location again. With the change in background, the fish assumed subtle color changes, almost perfectly camouflaged.

The octopus is amazingly adaptive. Not only is the creature highly intelligent, it is also able to change color rapidly to foil attackers and blend in with the surroundings. Its flexible body can almost mold itself into rocks or crevices, then, except for the pulsing siphon, the octopus is perfectly hidden. If disturbed an ink gland exudes a black smoke screen as the octopus darts off.

Cryptic behavior or cryptic coloration describes the situation where an organism blends with its background. The animal chooses a background that matches its color or behaves like the background to avoid detection. The animals do not change color themselves.

One example of cryptic behavior is typified by the trumpetfish. When threatened, the thin, needlelike fish seeks out an anchor line, thin branch of coral, or anything long and angular and simply stands on its head, vertical in the water, motionless, simulating the background. The creature hunts its food in the same way. Waiting motionless, blending in with its background, the trumpetfish waits for

Perfectly motionless, a baby trumpet fish has positioned its long, narrow body vertically along a piece of gorgonia coral. Able to remain perfectly still, the trumpetfish uses its adaptive behavior to elude predation.

prey to come within easy reach.

Trumpet fish exist in a variety of colors. Bright yellow trumpets are common in Hawaii while their mottled grayish blue relatives occur in Florida and the Caribbean. Often, a number of different varieties of trumpetfish live in the same environment.

The way some of these creatures adhere to their disguises underwater is amazing. I've often seen little trumpet fish line themselves up with a diver's arm or even his regulator hose or tank, remaining vertical, motionless and moving along with the background. Sometimes a diver will purposefully move the critters normal cover and substitute a hand, watching the little fish act out its pattern of cryptic behavior against the diver's outstretched fingers.

The little file fish is particularly well adapted to the charade it acts out against a background of gorgonian coral. The fanlike coral, with its striations and boxed pattern, provides a backdrop for this little creature that parks itself in a vertical position, remaining perfectly still. The fish's coloration and pattern enables it to match the coral background. If a diver slips his hand between the fish and the coral and then moves the coral out of the way, the cute little file fish will adhere to its pattern of cryptic behavior remaining vertical against the diver's hand.

51

Insistence on instinctive protective behavior, even in a changing environmental situation, may doom some of these amazing little creatures. Their cryptic behavior patterns or ability to change color have enabled them to adapt to their environment and thus survive.

Small differences are often noted among similar marine species that inhabit the same range underwater. As mentioned, it is rare in nature that an adaptation develops without a purpose. Sometimes the adaptation can be related to Gause's Law. This biological principle holds that two forms of life cannot occupy permanently the same ecological niche. It is therefore a matter of survival that a marine organism develops a special adaptation that enables it to alter its range in the living space, thus competing in a slightly different way.

The chronicle of adaptive changes among marine creatures is almost endless. The little, devil-may-care seahorse, *Hippocampus erectus*, can change the minute chromatophores in its skin to protective adaptations of brown, yellow, green, and orange, depending on the color of sea grasses in which they hide. Some sea horses have even developed eccentric branches from head and body. These little growths, resembling fringes, add to the disguise, making them look strangely like the environment in which they live.

Some fish change color at night, adapting to the darkness. An example is found with the spotted goatfish, *Pseupeneus maculatus*. Sporting dark blotches on its white body in the daylight, the splotches turn red at night. The blue tang, *Acanthurus coeruleus*, appearing plain dark blue in the daylight sea, puts on a gaudy array of stripes at night. Adapting to its night hunting, the Spanish grunt, *Haemulon macrostomum*, wears subdued patches of brown, while in the daylight it sports flagrant stripes.

I've spent many hours underwater observing the antics of the lizard fish. This small rascal, which looks curiously like its namesake, sits patiently on a piece of coral or wiggles itself down in the sand. Perfectly camouflaged, the lizard fish just waits its chance and pops out for lunch when a fish happens near. Lizard fish, too, appear in color and pattern variations, depending on their location. After observing its feeding scenario, I watched a lizard fish with half-devoured quarry in its mouth settle its body into the sand to placidly finish its meal. The lizard fish was almost completely concealed except for its mouth, full of fish, and eyes.

There are many species that resort to color change to avoid detection. Others bury themselves in the sand on the bottom. Some combine the two techniques like the flatfish we've described or any of a variety of rays or skates which possess the ability to change color.

This ability in a ray, which possesses potentially dangerous barbs, as we will see later, makes it incumbent on divers and swimmers to proceed with caution so as not to step on one accidentally. Bathers entering the water in the tropics often shuffle their feet in the sand to give the ray ample notice to get out of the way.

Color change in marine creatures may require a few hours or seconds depending on the animal. The change requires a complex coordination in the nervous system, which responds to visual patterns picked up by the fish's eye.

Eyes can be used in a different way, especially false eyes. To the delicate butterfly fish, a false set of eye spots near the tail and a misleading coloration around the head and tail, is enough to confuse a predator long enough for the little fish to get away. The fishy set of spots, resembling eyes, gives the delicious tidbit the impression of a head at the wrong end. The disguise works just fine. Underwater I've observed a grouper charge for the wrong end of a butterfly fish, anticipating the intended victim would escape forward. The clever little prey scooted easily away in the opposite direction, real eye first.

Bizzare and blaring stripes often aid small reef fish in evading predators. The array of color and zebralike stripes with confusing patterns near the head and tail are often just enough to give the little victim a fraction of a second to get away. It's that slight edge that means the difference between survival and death.

Some highly adapted marine organisms actually fish for their food. The angler fish, *Phrynelox scaber*, or its cousin, the tropical Atlantic sargassumfish, *Histrio histrio*, are eccentric-looking creatures resembling lumps bedecked with seaweed or fronds. Lying still, they almost defy detection, so ornately do their skin fronds and branches resemble the vegetation and surroundings in which they live. Angler fish are equipped with a feeler topped by a fleshy lure, extending from their forehead. By wiggling the lure, the angler fish brings prey to within a centimeter of its mouth. The rest is digestion. Other species that have developed this angle for luring prey by means of a built-in fishing pole include the angling turtle, *Macrollemmus temmincki*, and a variety of catfish called *Chala chala*.

In a rather exotic mimicry of a friendly fish, which is known to be beneficial to its temporary host, enjoying a symbiotic relationship with it, the sabre-toothed blenny, *Aspidontus taeniatus*, looks, acts, and behaves like the cleaner wrasse, *Labroides dimidiatus*. Most skin divers have seen fish in tropical waters stopping off at a cleaning station manned by little blue, purple, black, and white cleaner wrasses.

53

There is nothing but peace and tranquility at these cleaner stations, as natural enemies wait their turn, calmly respecting the neutrality of the station. The cleaner wrasses themselves would, under other circumstances, be eaten by the larger fish. In the cleaner stations they are allowed to move freely about the predatious giant's mouth, picking minute parasites from the teeth, jaws and gills of the larger fish, performing an important service. It's all neutrality and charm while the big fish enjoy their paracure.

The mimic blenny, looking almost exactly like the helpful cleaner wrasse, swims up behind the big fish, happily enthralled by the atmosphere in his beauty parlor. Waiting its chance, the impostor bites out a little chunk of the big fish's tail. The large fish, rousted from his tranquility and shocked that anything like this should happen at a cleaner station, whirls around to attack whatever it was that dined off its tail. The impostor blenny simply stays in the same place, acting totally innocent like the real beneficial fish, remaining unmolested in his cleaner wrasse costume. The larger fish would never suspect a helpful cleaner wrasse of doing such a nasty thing, after all.

THE STING

In some cases nature combines a creature's camouflage with a deadly potential. Venomous marine animals account for some of the strangest adaptations in the oceans.

I was diving in the South Pacific when one of the student divers I had below began signaling frantically. He was pointing to a piece of coral. I peered under the rocky formation. Underneath, in the hollow recession under the coral, a lion fish, *Pterois radiata*, armed spines deployed for action, was hanging upside down. The diver was holding his wrist, so we surfaced.

On board the boat, I examined the diver's hand. He had been stung on one finger. The finger and knuckle had swollen to double the normal size. He complained of extreme localized pain. The diver said that there had been some slight bleeding underwater from the site of the puncture wound.

The injury was typical of many that occur each year. A diver accidentally puts his hand or foot on a poisonous fish underwater, or a swimmer accidentally steps on the deadly spines. For the diver in my party, the accident was not too serious. He was treated by soaking the wound in very hot water (60°C), which acts to break down the protein-based venom. Topical antiseptic and antihistamine and antiinflammatory cream on the cleansed wound prevented reaction to the venom, and overnight the diver's pain and symptoms disappeared.

As with the vast majority of potentially dangerous creatures, venomous marine animals are not aggressive toward man. Languid and relatively immobile, they often barely move even when disturbed, depending in large measure on their natural camouflage for protection. It is only by accident that a person is injured by them. The highly specialized coloring and body patterns that enable these fish to remain so well camouflaged in their environment make them especially fascinating to study.

The stone fish, *Synanceja verrucosa*; scorpion fish, *Scorpaena gibbosa* and *Scorpaenopsis diabolus*; and lion fish, dragon fish, or turkey fish, *Pteoris volitans* and *Pterois radiata* among others, are all potentially deadly. The common names for these varieties amply describe their fashion of camouflage and behavior.

Each year in French Polynesia alone, the stone fish, *Synanceja verrucosa*, is responsible for about eighty injuries involving man. Although no fatality has been reported in the literature in Polynesia, or disclosed from my interviews with physicians on the islands, the Australian stone fish have indeed caused several deaths.

Stone fish venom is injected into the wound by means of dorsal, pelvic, and anal spines. Some spines have been measured to lengths of 9.8 mm. Canals run along the spines from poison glands just under the skin which transmit the venom. When a bather or diver inadvertently steps or puts his hand down on a spine, the pressure is sufficient to depress the integument layer covering it and cause the venom to move up the canal and be injected into the wound.

The severity of the wound and subsequent poisoning is directly correlated to the size of the stone fish. Some of the larger varieties, attaining lengths of and exceeding 25 cm., are capable of injecting a lethal dose of poison.

Appropriately named, the stone fish is perfectly camouflaged in its environment. They occur in a variety of colors and are found among rocks and coral formations. That perfect camouflage enables the stone fish to remain perfectly still in its environment, gulping down fish that happen by in front of its mouth. This perfect camouflage also accounts for most of the accidental woundings to swimmers and divers. Occasionally fishermen are stricken while untangling the stone fish from their nets.

Depending on the number of punctures and the amount of venom injected, most victims exhibit immediate violent pain radiating the length of the affected member, accompanied by swelling. The wound itself may bleed from the site of the puncture. Often unconsciousness results, and frequently cardiac and neurological complications make a wound from the stone fish potentially fatal. Stone and lion fish venom is thermolabile, or destroyed by heat since it is a protein-based poison. Immediate immersion of the wound in 60°C hot water containing laundry bleach may serve to break the poison down. Hospital treatment involves the use of antistone fish serum that is manufactured in Australia and hard to come by in most remote areas.

Even for the trained observer, so well disguised are these stone fish that they often go unnoticed. I was diving with a companion in Tahiti, engrossed in my picture taking. Suddenly my diving buddy held my leg to keep it from moving. Looking around, I saw that my leg had come to rest right next to a stone fish. I remembered swimming past it without paying any attention, figuring it was actually just a piece of the bottom.

Once located, I've found stone fish to be relatively territorial. Over one patch of reef in Polynesia, where I dove each day for almost a six-month period, the same stone fish would be on or near their reef each time I paid a visit. Since they were so dependable, I used the two to show new divers, and, as models, they posed for innumerable pictures.

One day a diver that had just learned the sport, came up from his dive rather excited. He scrambled up on the dock and proudly displayed one of my "pet" stone fish impaled on a screwdriver. The diver thought he was performing a public service, rather than interfering with the stable composition of reef life and depriving others of the opportunity to observe and photograph the fish in its habitat.

The scorpion fish, *Scorpaena gibbosa, S. diabolus* and other varieties account for a number of stings each year in tropical waters. Resembling in many respects the stone fish, scorpion fish too conceal themselves amid rocks and coral. Although the venom in the spines is nowhere near as toxic as the stone fish, scorpion fish wounds can cause severe pain and sometimes complications from allergic reactions.

Among the most beautiful and exotic-looking creatures in the sea are the lion fish, zebra fish, turkey fish, or dragon fish, *Pterois volitans, P. radiata* and others. Brightly colored and ornamental with gaily decorated spines, the fish live among coral, usually nestling on the underside of rocky recessions underwater. They inhabit caves and grottoes which provide them with shelter during the day. These species leave the protection of their homes at night to feed.

The spines of *Pterois* are long and slender, capable of being moved about freely. *P. volitans* is reddish brown in color, and the flexible

An aura of mystery surrounds the exploration of any shipwreck. Here in Micronesia dozens of ships were sunk during the battle of Truk Lagoon. So still are the armaments of war, now overgrown with colorful sponges and encrustations of coral, that a filmmaker for National Geographic commented that nature has turned the "guns into garlands." This photograph shows the author exploring the bow gun of a ship.

Photographing sharks in their natural habitat can be a tricky and dangerous undertaking. A Tahitian diver and fisherman guided the author to some caves where small white tip reef sharks, like the one captured in this picture, were sleeping in the caves. For a long time it was believed that sharks never slept, continually swimming to keep from sinking. This myth persisted in spite of observations of "sleeping sharks" made by free divers and spear fishermen, who discovered sharks lying placidly under rock formations and in caves, like this small white tip.

While diving off the island of Rangiroa in the Tuamotus, the author photographed this Manta Ray swimming with remoras attached to its underside. The Manta had a wing span of almost fifteen feet from tip to tip and was accompanied everywhere by the voracious remoras. The remora attaches itself to the underside of a fish or ray by means of a flat suction plate on the top of its head. While the benefit to the host is often unclear, the remoras derive a definite benefit from the relationship, using the host for protection and feeding off the scraps churned up or spurned in the host animal's feeding.

Coral polyps extend their delicate tentacles out of the hard calcium carbonate theca or cup to draw minute particles of plankton into their oral cavity. Often the tentacles only extend at night to feed, making a night dive full of color not visible during the day. The undulation of the tentacles draws the plankton into the oral cavity.

A small flatfish or sole, sporting fringes and camouflage colors, has wiggled its body into the sand and lies almost perfectly concealed on the bottom. Many varieties of flounder and fluke have minute chromatophores in their integument which enable them to change color at will. This natural disguise serves both for protection against predators and also to give the fish an advantage in hunting its food.

This picture of a so-called turkey fish, *Pterois volitans*, was taken off the coast of the Philippines. Each of the spines is capable of injecting a venom which is potentially fatal to humans allergic to the poison. Nonaggressive, the turkey fish is usually seen lying placidly on the bottom. When provoked the fish turns itself vertically in the water, deploying its spines in self-defense.

These marine algae resemble bunches of grapes. They are said to be of an edible variety, but their taste is not going to make them an overnight gustatory success. The picture was taken in shallow water in the Pacific, off the coast of Uman Island.

Seaweed (marine algae) grows in the shallow reaches of the ocean where light is abundant. Marine plants produce oxygen, provide shelter for smaller fish and marine life and are the staple diet of smaller animals, later consumed themselves by those higher-up in the food chain.

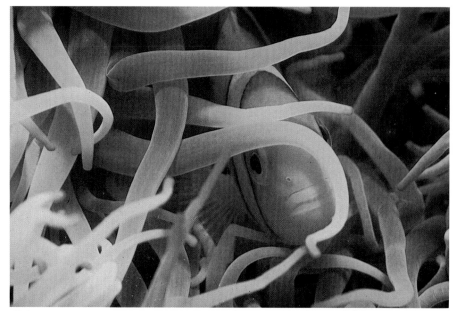

This sea anemone is carnivorous. Its stinging tentacles trap and paralyze small fish that venture near, often lured within range by the small clown fish, *Amphiprion chrysopterus*. The most current scientific thought as to why the clown fish is able to swim in and out of the stinging tentacles, seemingly immune to their poison, is that it has developed a secretion on its skin that does not provoke the anemone's tentacles to discharge their stinging nematocysts. In return for attracting unassuming prey within range of the stinging tentacles, the clown fish receives protection and feeds off left-overs.

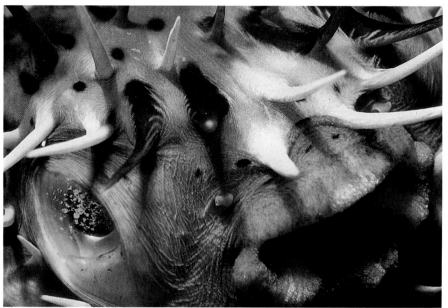

When threatened, a puffer fish has the ability to swallow water to inflate its body often to the size of a basketball. The sharp spines which are adaptations developed from scales, deter predation. Puffers, considered by some to be a gourmet treat and aphrodisiac, contain a deadly poison that attacks the central nervous system.

Feather duster worms, their beautiful and delicate plumes extended for feeding, filter small particles from the water and direct them toward the stoma or oral cavity. At the slightest vibration or stimuli, the feather dusters are immediately pulled back into the protective shelter of their tubelike homes, only to extend again when the danger is past.

Small shrimp like this *Periclimenes*, only about an inch long, enjoy the protection of a sea anemone. The anemone provides a protected shelter for the little shrimp which lures prey within range of the tentacles.

At the upper portion of the Congo River, fishermen sling hand-made wooden traps to catch large river fish. For whole tribes, fishing means survival. Families barter or sell fish they do not consume in order to buy necessary household goods. Primitive fishing techniques and lack of refrigeration insure a kind of conservation that will enable the river to sustain tribal life.

Arab dhow caught in the sudden violence of a storm. A member of the crew has been swept overboard and is struggling to regain the boat.

spines often sport maroon, brown, red, and white coloring. The venom is produced in hollow cavities along the spines. The spines do not inflict a deep wound, and very little venom is required because it is highly toxic. Although the diver in Tahiti experienced only localized pain and swellling, complications may include respiratory failure, shock, cardiac failure, and cyanosis (turning blue from lack of oxygen).

Prevalent throughout the Pacific, some of the most exotic looking turkey fish, a colorful description of these creatures, were living on the bamboo traps of Philippino fishermen in Batangas on the South China Sea. There were dozens of the fish, resting on the bamboo debris where the old traps had rotted and new bamboo supports were sunk. The water dropped off rapidly, with the bamboo supports sunk in depths exceeding 160 feet. Most of the turkey fish seemed to be at about 90 to 100 feet. The colony of them were quite at home on the old fish traps, the debris providing an artificial reef attracting small fish and other marine life upon which the turkey fish could feed. The "bamboo reef" colony seemed relatively communal and unless disturbed, rather sedentary.

Lion fish, dragon fish, and turkey fish are found throughout tropical waters. Their common names are derived from their color patterns. In the waters of the South Pacific, *Pterois* generally lives in small recessions in or under the coral or in small caves. It is common to observe four or five of them squatting together, hanging upside down, spines flayed out. At night the little fish move out on the reef to feed but rarely wander far from their caves. When provoked, the fish generally try to find shelter in a crevice or recession in the coral and aim their spines outward defensively. If the little lion fish is pursued, then it may deploy its spines somewhat like a porcupine, aiming them in the direction of the antagonist and make short advances to try to sting its foe or the snorkel or hand of the curious diver.

In addition to color-changing and camouflage abilities, certain rays in the *Myliobatidae* and *Dasyatidae* families possess caudal spines which are capable of inflicting nasty wounds. The spotted eagle ray or leopard ray, *Aetobatis narinari*, with its thick body and doglike face, accounts for most of the accidental woundings to humans in the Pacific.

Fishermen or swimmers wading into shallow water, over sand, can receive a sting from the dartlike barbs in the ray's tail. Venomous glands along the dart's holster, between the dermis and epidermis, secrete poison over the surface of the spine or dart. Minute barbules on the spine itself not only cause severe lacerations but also promote the spread of the toxin.

The darts or spines are defensive mechanisms. Rays make every effort to avoid contact with man. Injuries have been reported to fishermen transporting wounded rays, and, in one rare reported case, death resulted from a sting ray wound to the victim's thorax. Although often exaggerated in folk lore, some injuries have been reported due to rays "throwing" their darts.

Sting ray wounds are quite painful and often involve the lymph glands, with occasional respiratory distress, paralysis, and unconsciousness. Medical attention includes soaking the wound in hot water to break the venom down and cleansing the wound. Antitetanus serum is also recommended.

Although some of the serious consequences to man have been discussed, it is clear that none of the animals in this section are aggressive toward man. They are basically passive, using their venom for defense, often just resting in the sand or coral, enjoying the protection their color or behavior pattern affords them. When man is injured, it is usually only the result of his own carelessness, an accident or where he has tried to capture or pursue the animal. The rule that is drilled into divers new to waters where they may encounter unfamiliar marine life is: "Look, but don't touch." If the underwater tourist wants to observe any of these particularly well adapted and artfully camouflaged marine organisms that are also venomous, that rule has to be amended slightly to: "Look carefully, but don't touch."

So limitless are the ways in which adaptations have enabled creatures to survive in their environment that one with an keen sense of observation and an appreciation for the gentle harmony in nature can discover a subtle world of fascination, learning how each creature blends with his milieu. One cannot help but wonder why man has so often insisted he is not a part of this harmony. It's all around us; each creature, in its own way, has managed to survive and adapt to its environment even as the environment changes around it. Adaptive coloration and behavior is a lesson nature has put in our path to stumble over and think about. Man, the most adapted and adaptive creature, hardly blends at all.

5

Ocean Resources

One thing becomes evident to the serious underwater explorer: Ocean resources are concentrated in the shallows, near the surface or around isolated underwater islands that stand out like desert oases, blossoming with life, surrounded by sand.

As in the terrestrial ecological system, plants in the ocean provide the essential nutrients for higher forms of life. Marine algologist Sylvia Earle has often remarked, "Most divers are not in the least interested in algae. . . . They ask how could I be interested in algae when there is so much else in the sea." In response, Sylvia put together a series of slides featuring her favorite plants. With total indifference to fish watchers, she regales divers with tales of algae power. Sylvia Earle's point is well taken. Plants in the sea, like their terrestrial counterparts, form and limit the ocean's ability to support higher forms of life.

PLANKTON

Phytoplankton, derived from two Greek words, phyton meaning plant and planktos meaning to wander or drift, is a general classification describing numerous species of small microscopic marine plants. These tiny single-celled plants synthesize more than 90% of the organic matter that supports ocean life. Phytoplankton production occurs on or near the surface where ample sunlight enables photosynthesis to take place.

The important role of plankton becomes evident when we consider that large marine plant life, the attached plants, can only exist in shallow water over continental shelves, near shoals, atolls, or shorelines. In total, this limits these larger plant forms to only about 2% of the world's entire ocean area.

Plankton flourish only in areas of the ocean with sufficient nutrients to support them. Nutrients reach the surface by upwellings in the sea floor. Upwellings stir up the bottom, bringing organic matter which had settled there, up toward the surface.

The existence of phytoplankton depends on this nutrient supply and sunlight. Since the phytoplankton support all other life, the higher forms that exist in a given ocean area are dependent on the availability of these tiny plants. One biologist drew an analogy to a farmer calculating how many cows he could pasture on his acreage.

Phytoplankton nutrient supplies may be artificially increased by dumping sewage waste or by changing the water conditions provoking a favorable climate for algal bloom, as occurs with power-plant thermal discharges. These artificially created algal blooms may be harmful to the overall ocean ecology, as will be discussed later. In normal ocean situations, upwellings of bottom matter occur when ocean currents change direction. Natural upwelling over shoals, such as those of the Grand Banks, takes place where deep ocean currents collide with geological faults or mountains that rise toward the surface. As the currents encounter this undersea topography, they "upwell" and carry rich nutrients off the bottom with them. The presence of plankton supporting nutrients provides a base for a whole ecological system of phytoplankton producers and smaller animal organisms which feed off the plankton. The system of upwelling supports the phytoplankton which are in turn consumed by zooplankton, or small drifting animal creatures, eaten by small fish which attract larger fish. The rich upwelling on the fishing grounds of the Grand Banks accounts for the good catch over these shoals.

Forces created by the spin of the Earth in its orbit also affect the currents and cause them to turn away from land. These coriolis forces, exerting influence on the ocean currents, create upwellings and the mixing of nutrients in surface layers.

The ocean is divided into zones by depth. The shallow littoral zone near shore includes the intertidal areas and wetlands. The shallowest ocean layer is called the Euphotic zone. This layer contains most of the ocean's marine life including plankton, small fish, and the larger predatory fish. The Mesopelagic zone, extending into the mid-range of the deep ocean, is inhabited by a variety of worms, giant squid, and lantern fish. The Bathypelagic zone houses wild-looking viper fish, angler fish, and gulpers. The abyssal deep ocean area is called the Benthic zone. The Benthic bottom is inhabited by crinoids, bristle starfish, sponges, lamp shells, and even bottom-dwelling fish called grenadiers.

It is in the uppermost layers of the sea that life cycles are cast for the entire ocean. Organic matter formed in these surface layers fuel the ocean's larger creatures. The residue of this ocean life, eventually tumbling down into the abyss, provides deep ocean dwellers with food. The settling debris becomes part of the sediment. As this material breaks down, some of it is recycled by upwellings. These upwellings of organic life rekindle the cycle, becoming nutrients for phytoplankton.

Taxonomists have compiled a list of more than two hundred thousand distinct species of plants and animals which exist in the seas and oceans. As science expands its view, as remote areas of the ocean are being explored, hundreds of new species are being discovered and added to this list each year.

Of the small varieties of marine phytoplankton, the cocolithophores are among the most common. They are motile and have a miniscule drop of oil inside their bodies which aids their buoyancy and stores food. Still microscopic in size but larger than some cocolithophores are the diatoms. These marine phytoplankton are encased in silica and rotate using flagella attached to their bodies. Nannoplankton describes many groups of the smallest phytoplankton, the word nanno meaning dwarf.

Herbivorous animal plankton is called zooplankton. These zooplankton consume phytoplankton, enlarging the food chain as they are in turn consumed by fish or higher forms of life. One group, the copepods, contain about 10,000 different species. Some species of copepods eat other zooplankton as well as phytoplankton, even consuming waste products of other organisms.

The best known of the copepods provide the mainstay of the baleen whale diet, krill. These krill or euphausiids, resemble small shrimp and are high in protein value.

The relationship between zooplankton and phytoplankton and between these planktonic forms and their consumers is complex. The relationships depend on many variable factors in the environment. In some areas the growth of phytoplankton follows seasonal changes, blooming with the availability of additional nutrients. Sudden changes occur, often without explanation, which account for changes in usual patterns of algal growth.

An environmental economist could well spend years analyzing the consequences of change involving plankton bloom. A historian could equate the algal bounty to the prosperity derived from rich fishing harvests. The richer the fishing, the greater the prosperity of some nations. One example that illustrates this economic impact involves the herring fishery.

Herring feed on zooplankton. While delectable to many human palates in the North country and popular smoked and pickled throughout the world, herring are especially important as food fish for larger species. The herring fishery, in fact the entire fishing industry, flourished in the Baltic Sea in the twelfth century. The little herring brought great prosperity to the cities in northern Germany. These cities flourished for about three hundred years until about the time the herring disappeared. As the herring fishery declined, most probably the result of a decline in plankton, these great cities declined economically.

It will require more research to undertake a complete analysis of the decline of this once great Hanseatic League, but certainly an important cause was the disappearance of these fickle fish. Our algologist friend, Sylvia Earle, would have it that the herring were only the proximate cause, the real reason was a decline in tiny marine plants. Perhaps she would be right.

Zooplankton are occasional travelers in the open oceans. Rarely do they amass except in areas of high nutrient content near shore or over shoals. Many forms of zooplankton assume intricate forms, some extending many feet in length. These zooplankton catch their food in mucus strands or jellylike wings. Very little research has been conducted on zooplankton in their natural environment. Most scientists see them only in tanks installed on research vessels or in the laboratory. The delicate webs and intricate adaptive mechanisms used to catch their food are usually destroyed in the netting process. As a result, since few researchers have donned scuba gear to observe these zooplankton in the open ocean, there is scant information about how these animals behave in the wild.

Salps, zooplankton in transparent barrel shapes, sometimes join together in long chains. Some varieties like the siphonophores stay in deeper water during the day, surfacing at night to feed on plants or animal plankton. Siphonophores use tiny gas sacks to accomplish this rising and sinking in the ocean. Trailing long stingers, the siphonophores may reach 60 to 100 feet in length.

SEAWEED AND GRASSES

Higher forms of marine plants are most often attached to a substrate. This means that they are restricted to relatively shallow water where sunshine can penetrate to permit photosynthesis. More complex marine algae, some attaining enormous size, are among the most dominant elements in the shallow underwater environment. The kelps for example, attain lengths of as much as 300 feet.

On land, larger plants are for the most part flowering, vascular plants that reproduce by the production of seeds. One thing is evident to the diver, while some huge kelps stand out because of their size, most marine plants are small. Marine algae are nonvascular, depending on the water to support them. The only vascular, flowering plants in the oceans are the grasses, save for rooted mangroves.

Vascular marine grasses have conductive tissue to transmit water throughout the plant (xylem) and conductive tissue to translocate food (phloem). These Anthophyta, anthos meaning flower, of the sea contain eight genera and about forty-five species. Shallow, inshore reaches of the ocean are dominated by the eel grass and turtle grass. These grasses, probably the most familiar to divers who go off sandy beaches, are members of the flowering marine plant group.

Marine grasses reproduce sexually, their seeds a favorite food of ducks and geese. Stems, roots and leaves, absent in marine algae, are present in the marine grasses. Larger flowering marine plants, like the mangroves, are rooted in the shallows, extending branches above the surface.

Phycologists classify marine algae by color. While all marine algae contain chlorophyll and produce food by photosynthesis, other pigments may dominate. The dominant color accounts for their classification as blue green, brown, golden brown, red, and yellow.

Blue green algae are individually very small plants, most often seen covering rocks, boat-launching ramps, or pier pilings. The blue green algae are responsible for causing divers to slip and fall getting into or out of the water.

There are over 900 species of green marine algae. The green algae range in size from individual plants invisible to the naked eye to

Marine algae provide the "staff of life" for an underwater environment. Here green algae grow between tiny yellow sponges.

varieties as large as 2 feet. Chlorophyll is the dominant pigment in green algae. Their scientific name is Chlorophycophyta, chloros meaning green, phykos a Greek word for seaweed, and phyton meaning plant. Many of the green algae are eaten by man.

The brown algae, called Phaeophycophyta, contain fucoxanthin. This accessory pigment gives them their brown color. There are about 1500 known individual species of brown algae that exist in the ocean environment. This classification includes tiny specimens, less than 2 or 3 millimeters in size, ranging up to the 300-foot-long kelps. Brown algae have an important economic value, used as organic fertilizer and processed into a wide variety of food products and fillers. Algin, produced from kelp plants, is used in medicines, cosmetics, beer, even toothpaste. The larger brown algae harbor a wide variety of life. Small marine creatures grow on the algae, spawn and lay their eggs in the shelter of the plants. Some marine creatures play among the kelp, using them as a point of orientation.

There are about 4000 marine Rhodophycophyta. These red (rhodo) algae have a filamentous body. Rhodophycophyta are used principally in the production of agar, a substance employed on petri plates for bacterial cultures in the laboratory. Red seaweeds are consumed in salads and made into tasty soups.

In many parts of the world, seaweed is a popular food. It is high in nutrients and readily available. Projects to cultivate certain popular seaweeds have been quite successful. Harvesting seaweed increases the productivity of the beds. The cutting of stalks permits light to penetrate. One variety of seaweed accumulates on the surface in an area of the Atlantic named for this phenomenon, the Sargasso Sea. In this large ocean area around Bermuda, where life is pushed together by countervailing currents and winds, the sargassum weed teems with life. The floating patches of weed become a point of orientation in mid-ocean. Sargasso weeds are supported on the surface by gas-filled sacks. The sargassum plays host to specialized life forms that camouflage themselves in the weed. Many of these crabs and fish resemble their environment so as to make them virtually undetectable. Whenever a handful of sargasso weed is removed from the sea and shaken, scores of tiny creatures can be seen scurrying out of their homes. Each handful of sargassum is a small ecosphere teeming with life.

FISH

For many people the psychological word relation test for ocean would be fish and for the word fish, ocean. The sea is perceived as a haven for fish and fish perceived abounding in the oceans. In most areas of the world, save the most affluent, fish are a mainstay of life. Commercial fishery statistics show that the world harvest of marine fishes in 1938 was about 20 million tons. In 1948 the commercial harvest was about 19.6 million tons, in 1963 about 46 million tons were taken, and in 1969 about 55 million tons of fish were caught. From 1850 to 1950, the catch of fish in the world increased tenfold and has averaged 25 percent more every 10 years.

If one were to extrapolate these figures against agricultural production, the fishery industry has had twice the increase of food harvested from the land. Experts estimate that, where photosynthesis is possible and plant nutrients abound, the ocean can produce more than 60 kilograms of fish per hectare each year. Fisheries' economists estimate that the oceans theoretically could yield more than 200 million tons of fish annually. This is only theoretical, assuming husbandry, ideal conditions, and the use of species not presently fished commercially.

Statistics relating world fishery harvests are somewhat misleading.

Classically, finicky tastes have meant that much of the harvest is not used as human food. Fish considered trash fish have been wasted or converted into meal. In the 1940s only about 10% of the entire harvest was used for meal. Today probably half of the world fishery harvest is consumed and half made into fish meal and used to feed livestock.

If one were to conduct a poll at the supermarket, asking customers to name fish they buy and eat, the result would probably end in a compilation of maybe a half-dozen fish. The list would probably include cod, flounder, salmon, bass, tuna in cans (fresh tuna is delicious eating, but many shoppers avoid it fresh, choosing the canned variety), canned sardines, and occasionally a tin of anchovies.

Many of the slick disguises and fancy names fish mongers have invented for skate, dogfish, or other unpopular items still have not popularized them among shoppers. A fishing enterprise, like any enterprise for profit, will respond to the market. Selective fishing has become popular. Boats are rigged out to pursue one particular kind of fish. When other fish are netted, they are frequently disgarded, often dead or so injured in the netting process that they die once returned to the water.

At the fish market, consumers are most attracted to what they can cook and lay before the family at dinner. This means the fish must be a certain size to be commercially viable. Smaller fish are rarely pursued by American commercial fishermen. They are not commercially feasible, harder to catch in equipment designed for larger species, and more fragile, requiring special handling.

The closer the fished species is to the producer level, the more efficient the net yield of usable energy-convertible food. This is not much different from what terrestrial ecologists have been saying about the rather inefficient process of raising beef cattle. The problem remains trying to interest consumers in alternative food sources. There have been promising results, however, diverting the philosophy just short of the human consumer level.

Anchovies, which graze directly on phytoplankton and thus are a highly efficient source of protein, have been ground up and used as feed for chickens. When their use as chicken feed created a viable market, fishermen pursued the small anchovy. Analyzing the impact of anchovy fishing, economists concluded that more protein was generated using the anchovies to feed the chickens than would have been generated had tuna eaten the anchovies and man eaten the tuna.

Trying to extrapolate fishery data, I came across some interesting statistics about California's sardine industry. In 1937, sardines caught in the Pacific off California set a world record. In that year, fishermen netted 791,000 tons of sardines. This was about 25% of the entire United States fish catch. Ten years before, the yield was only about 50,000 tons per year. In the years following 1937, the sardines declined drastically until only a little over one thousand tons were taken in the sixties. Presently the California sardine fishery is considered almost nonexistent, a sad memorial to a failure to husband ocean resources.

Oddities occur in ocean fisheries that seemingly have no explanation. More precisely, the natural cause has not been discovered. Grand Banks fishermen traditionally took cod, eating part of their catch. In 1879, a cod fisherman hooked a species that hadn't been seen before. They cooked it up on board, found it quite tasty, and brought the fish to market. These tile fish were so well received that over the next three years they were fished commercially. For some reason, not completely understood or explained, in the spring of 1882, fishermen found tile fish dead over 5000 square miles of traditional fishing grounds. They estimated that a billion of them were floating dead on the surface. It has been theorized that changes in water temperature killed the fish which showed no signs of toxic poisoning or physical damage. No tile fish were caught that year and fishermen began to think they were extinct. The tile fish mysteriously disappeared and were not seen again until 1892 when eight were caught. Thereafter, tile fish began to appear again and in 1935 about 2 1/2 million pounds were caught. In the early 1960s, the annual tile fish catch was about 3/4 million pounds.

The Pacific pollock has become a popular food fish in Japan. It feeds on copepods, amphipods and krill. The pollock is low on the food chain thus a highly efficient protein source, existing in great numbers in Alaska's plankton rich Bering Sea. The taking of pollock is only a recent innovation for fishermen who ignored pollock in favor of yellowfin sole taken in the same waters. Around 1960, Japanese and Russian trawlers began catching massive numbers of sole. They caught 400,000 metric tons where sustainable yields were 100,000 metric tons per year. As a result, the sole dwindled, until by 1963, the combined Russian and Japanese sole harvest was only about 50,000 metric tons. This massive overfishing depleted the sole population causing the Russians and Japanese to focus on pollock which could be caught in the same area with the same fishing gear.

Mother ships with fleets of fishing vessels now sought out the plankton-eating pollock in great numbers. In one year, twelve

Japanese "factory" vessels operated in the Bering Sea with a retinue of fourteen catchers each along with forty-two independent fishing trawlers. The combined Pacific pollock catch taken by Japanese and Russian ships amounted to about 1 1/2 million metric tons per year.

The pollock fishery, which has been in operation only since the 1960s is already in danger from overharvesting. Consumer preference in the United States ran to cod fish. The price of cod went up 70% in one year (1973). As a consequence, the pollock, poor cousin to the cod, was imported from Japan. Imports of pollock rose from around 800 metric tons in 1971 to about 20,000 metric tons in 1973, the year the price of cod fish skyrocketed.

The new demand put greater pressure on the diminishing stocks. The Japanese maintained a steady harvest in the Bering Sea only by increasing the intensity of fishing effort and by tracking pollock by sonar. The sole were wiped out. All sizes of sole were now caught in the pollock trawls. The pollock caught were no longer optimum adult size. Their average dropped from about 15 to 16 inches (caught in 1971) to only about a foot in 1974. In addition, the overharvesting resulted in a decline in fishing efficiency. The per hour catch fell off 75%.

Controls were too late and too little. Governments and fishermen competed for dwindling fish stocks in the Bering Sea. The story of the Pacific pollock is not a completed tale for the fishery still exists. This situation is, however, a clear example of the effect overfishing can have in depleting and destroying a species' ability to reproduce in a relatively short time.

The same plight has befallen the haddock fishery on Georges Bank. Calculations show that the same amount of haddock can be taken if 25% of the vessels are removed from the fleet. Optimal fishing efficiency would be realized if 50% were removed. Fishermen compete for dwindling stocks, expending more money on the pursuit of less fish.

When government intervenes to protect the vanishing species, they usually impose controls that only serve to aggravate the problem: Fishing seasons and hours, types of rigs that can be deployed, size of ships. This renders the pursuit of fish more costly and intensifies the competition. If a fishing season is limited or quotas imposed, captains will put on more ships and race to get the fishing in before the quotas are reached or the season closed. That is the nature of fierce competition. It is also wasteful. It makes little sense to decrease the efficiency or profitability of a fishing operation. Fishermen hurry to catch yellowfin tuna in the Pacific before the season closes. Then they push on to fish the Atlantic where the season is still open or switch to other species. In an overly competitive situation, a fisherman who has put four boats on the water to get the most out of a limited season cannot realize a profit from his capital investment unless he can work his boats on other fishing grounds or take other species. More fish have to be taken to make the overall operation profitable. The problem is not easily solved. Equitable means must be devised to protect certain species from overfishing without penalizing the fishermen who must still earn a livelihood.

A friend of mine in the South Pacific had a profitable business going on the Tuamotu islands. He started a lobstering enterprise, diving for and trapping them. He would ice the catch and ship it off to Tahiti. My friend hired natives to work for him and the enterprise flourished. Others, seeing there was money to be made decided to go into the business. Many of the fishermen took baby lobsters and females with eggs. No one could tell any of them to stop. No one would listen to arguments that they were depleting the stocks of lobsters. Eventually, the lobsters were gone and the businesses collapsed. Overharvesting killed the enterprise that, had it been properly managed, could have been profitably conducted in perpetuity.

Reacting to the poor financial condition of the United States fishing industry, Congress enacted the Fishery Conservation and Management Act of 1976. This act extended territorial control over an exclusive fishery zone from the traditional 12 to 200 miles from shore. Information available showed that the annual U.S. catch remained static at 2 to 2.2 million tons, while American imports of fish tripled in twenty-five years, since 1959. This control zone extension, it was hoped, would give American fishermen a better crack at the estimated potential harvest of 20 to 40 billion pounds of fish off the U.S. Coastal zone. With Russian trawlers pressing close to American territorial water, Congress hoped the new law would give American fishermen the lion's share of the $12 billion potential resources off U.S. waters on the continental shelves. No matter who takes the profit, overfishing means there will be less fish to take and it will cost more per pound to take them. In the extreme case, fish stocks may be depleted entirely.

Part of the impetus for the passage of the Fishery Conservation and Management Act, extending America's 200-mile control zone over fisheries, was the gun boating of American trawlers in Peru and elsewhere. Peru, perhaps the largest fishing nation in the world with a fleet of more than 1900 trawlers, has claimed and enforced a 200-mile limit.

Part of the Peruvian fishing industry has its base in the rich anchovy harvest. The Peruvian anchoveta peaked at about 8 million tons per year. These anchovies are plant-plankton feeders. They thrive in cold, nutrient rich water coming up from the Antarctic with Peru's Humboldt Current. Anchovies provide food for Peru's 16 million sea birds. The birds dump nitrogen rich guano on islands where it is collected and sold as fertilizer. Guano interests effectively blocked anchovy fishing for a long time in order not to deprive the bird population of their staple. Anchovy fishing was drastically curtailed until chemical fertilizer replaced guano. It costs about $10 to $12 a ton to harvest the anchovies in Peru and even with a catch of 8 million tons, perhaps 3 million tons are still consumed by the birds. The Peruvians have found that if the annual anchovy harvest exceeds 10 million tons per year, the size of the anchovy caught decreases.

Environmental factors such as the southeast trade winds, cause upwellings of the water as it is driven north by the Humboldt Current. These upwellings enrich the water with nutrients, promoting the growth of plankton.

When the trade winds weaken, especially after an exceptionally hot summer, the upwellings cease. Warm water juts south down Peru's coast. This natural condition occurs every few years with devastating results. The plankton do not bloom and the anchovy do not appear. The warm water causes rainfall and floods along Peru's coastal towns, washing torrents of mud into the ocean. The Peruvians call this phenomenon *El Niño*, for it happens around Christmas time and is said to coincide with the coming of the Christ child. *El Niño* illustrates one aspect of the multiple and dynamic conditions that affect ocean fisheries.

It was only in March 1967, that the United States Food and Drug Administration withdrew its mandated labeling of fish meal. Prior to this time, the highly concentrated protein meal could only be shipped in containers labeled "unfit for human consumption in the United States." An odd regulation when one considers that protein for protein one ton of $3500 per ton tuna has the same food value as one ton of $12 per ton anchovy.

Over thousands of dives in Polynesia, the absence of large fish was apparent around many of the reefs. For the Polynesians, fishing meant subsistence. The larger islands were being called on more frequently by Japanese refrigerated ships. A generator-powered freezer was installed on Rangiroa. The island's fishermen were able to store fish in quantity for the first time.

This new refrigeration system changed the habits of the island. Previously, small wooden Tahitian boats set out from Papeete with ice. Their range was limited by the time it would take to get to the out islands and back before the ice melted. In this traditional way, there were always plenty of fish for the Polynesians to eat and sell at market to earn money for necessities.

With the advent of refrigeration and Japanese refrigerated ships, we could see the potential overharvesting coming. On the reefs, the rocks and coral were marked with nicks from spear-guns. Free divers regularly hunted the reefs for fish. The number of fast bonita boats fishing the deeper offshore areas increased.

A Tahitian friend no longer used the rocked-in pool he made in the lagoon, where he and his family traditionally kept extra fish alive until needed. My friend bought a freezer and began stocking and selling fish. Toward the end of my stay in Polynesia, my friend was complaining that he was not able to make the payments on his boat because the fish were not as plentiful. He said he could no longer catch enough. He thought he would do much better if he could manage a loan to get a second boat. He wanted to do what the other fishermen were doing. They bought three or four boats on credit and were selling to the Japanese. The Japanese would go home when there were no more fish to be bought in Polynesia. The Polynesians would starve.

SPEAR-FISHING

For the sport scuba diver today, vast educational opportunities present themselves for achievement in areas of photography and research, tending to deemphasize spear-fishing. On the whole, the taking of fish by sport spear-fishermen, selecting what they need for a meal or enjoying a beach barbeque of shellfish, will have little impact on overall ocean resources. On the other hand, spear-fishing contests that cause indiscriminate taking of fish not consumed by the hunter himself, sometimes even thrown away, are wasteful.

Most reef areas where spear-fishing contests take place are relatively stable. Reef species remain in the same general area for their entire lives. In these areas, concentrated over-spearing can decimate a reef community. Grouper, for example, take up residence in caves or underwater rock formations. Divers can return year after year to the same reefs. The grouper in residence, if left alone, will still be there, territorial as ever. After a world spear-fishing competition I observed in the Mediterranean, most of the grouper were killed. The caves where these elder denizens had lived were empty.

Deliberate overfishing by divers has partially accounted for

71

depletion of large tracks of the Mediterranean. The underwater environment is barren of large fish, including areas that even ten years ago had bountiful stocks. This depletion cannot all be blamed on divers with spear-guns. Pollution and traditional fishing played a major role in this depletion. Divers with spear-guns had a significant impact, however.

Sensitivity to ecological relationships is often sufficient to create environmental responsibility among scuba divers. No one who has come to explore the beauty of the underwater world, to see the relationships of creatures in the deep, would want to destroy these resources.

SEABED RESOURCES

The seabed under the world's oceans accounts for 71% of the Earth's surface area. Mineral resources on and under the seabed are being increasingly coveted as technological advances make ocean mining feasible and profitable. If these seabed resources could be mined with the same facility as land resources, they would be far more valuable than those that remain on land.

Sophisticated research ships, like the *Glomar Challenger*, are equipped to probe the ocean depths and recover objects from the deep ocean.

Among the resources on the seabed are phosphorites, a phosphate compound that is used as fertilizer. Obvious ocean resources of sand and gravel are used in construction, recovered from the shallows. Salt is removed from the ocean and sold commercially. Some cultures even use salt blocks as a form of currency in barter. In parts of Africa, I've seen camel caravans, laden with blocks of ocean salt, setting out for the interior where the commodity is highly valued in trade.

Many minerals have been recovered from the sea floor. Diamonds and deposits of gold have been found in South Africa, and tin has been dredged from the Gulf of Siam.

Manganese nodules abound in the deeper reaches of the Atlantic and Pacific Oceans. These irregular lumps of metal contain rich deposits of manganese, nickel, and cobalt. Manganese nodules are so numerous in some areas of the seabed that all that is required is equipment that can scoop them up from depths of about 12,000 feet. Private enterprise is awaiting resolution of the issue of ownership with the passage of a treaty under the International Law of the Sea, before full-scale operations begin.

There are many valuable minerals dissolved in sea water, including gold and precious metals. At present, technology does not exist to profitably extract these resources in commercial quantities.

Interests are scrambling for oil and gas reserves deep below the seabed floor. Production wells have blossomed. So many oil rigs now operate in the Gulf of Mexico that they impede navigation. In 1972 alone, approximately 3.5 thousand million barrels of oil and 184 thousand million cubic meters of natural gas were recovered from beneath the oceans. We will explore the pollution effects of this increased exploitation of oil and gas deposits under the seas in another chapter. Suffice to say here, however, that prices by oil-producing nations of oil recovered from land resources has increased the feasibility of sinking wells offshore. Exploration in the Atlantic off Atlantic City, New Jersey, has produced one promising well and exploration continues with high hopes. Britain has become self-sufficient in oil thanks to their North Sea wells off the coast of Scotland.

Debate continues over the effect of permitting exploration for oil in the Grand Banks fishing area. In this region, the likelihood of success in bringing in productive wells is fairly high. Fishermen oppose this exploration, fearing that an accident, like the blow out in the Bay of Campeche in the Gulf of Mexico, would destroy Grand Banks fishing.

There is great wealth in and under the oceans. Exploitation of these resources is the future hope of mankind. Careless abuse or reckless disregard for the balance that exists in nature will prevent the optimum utilization of these vital resources. If efforts are not made to conserve, husband, and protect the oceans, they will yield less, not more. Pollution, as we will see, only decreases the sea's capacity to support life, drastically reducing the harvest of food.

6

The Legacy of War

Vast reaches of the ocean floor, in fact most areas of the ocean bottom, are sandy deserts, incapable of supporting life. In nature, where there are limited habitats, having a suitable living space means survival. The territorial instinct of many animals underwater is easily observable, and often these fragile creatures engage in brave duels to protect and defend their homes, because for them it is a matter of life or death.

Hydrostructure may not be the word lexicographers settle on to define the construction of artificial submarine reefs, but it is a descriptive word I've coined to describe the seeding of the ocean floor with an artificial substrate to promote the growth of marine organisms.

Some of the earliest attempts at artificial reef building began with the helter-skelter dumping of scrap into the water. While effective on a short-term basis, these old refrigerators, air-conditioners, wrecked car bodies, and assorted discards disintegrated in time, causing the reef to collapse.

Used automobile tires, long the bane of an American society which generates an estimated 200 million of them each year, have proven a fairly effective substrate for building underwater reefs. Unlike metal, the tires, if weighted down and linked together, form a fairly long-lasting base material for reef building. Scrap tires are not the ideal substrate as foundation material for a coral reef, but as fishhavens they are readily available and cheap and serve a useful purpose. Some tire dealers accumulate the scrapped tires so fast they must pay to have them hauled away.

Weighted with stones, we used to sink these old tires in Long Island Sound or in the ocean, returning in a few months to see them encrusted with attaching organisms such as anemone, barnacles, and sponges. Playing our underwater lights around the inner recesses of the tires would usually produce a lobster in residence, proving that most anything can serve as an underwater homestead.

The fish didn't seem to care what scrap tenement they were moving into as long as it provided shelter and a protected niche for their eggs. The sponges and anemone never looked beyond the fact that the substrate was something they could attach to.

In order to control the dumping of alien materials into the oceans and other bodies of water, Congress passed the Marine Protection, Research and Sanctuaries Act of 1972. Under this law, certain safeguards and permit requirements insure that dumping of materials in the water will not unreasonably degrade or endanger human health or welfare or the marine environment. The act also establishes safeguards to protect the ecological systems and economic potential of the seas and oceans.

Internationally, many nations have begun seeding the ocean floor to create fishhavens and artificial reefs. In Australia, the Victoria Department of Fisheries and Wildlife has experimented with a variety of materials to determine what is best suited as a substrate. In Port Philip Bay at Melbourne, Australian officials have set out large numbers of cement-filled tires, connected in linked series. Australian fisheries experts have also designed cement pylons specifically for artificial reef construction. The pylons, resembling large toy jacks, have been assembled into reefs. Divers have reported that these pylons are very effective, and, since they are cast in cement, the pylons will provide a permanent base for the reefs. The one drawback to widespread use of the pylons is their high initial cost to manufacture and transport.

The fisheries scientists in Victoria have laid out four basic types of seeding materials: steel frames in the shape of cubes, quarry stone, cast concrete blocks, and old cement-weighted car tires.

To date experience has shown that over the long run, the best seeding materials for an artificial reef are those materials that are virtually indestructible and will not disintegrate with the effects of sea water. Among the best materials in those categories have been stone and cement.

Many researchers point to the success the Japanese have had artificially seeding the ocean with abalone, growing oysters, and harvesting fish. The consistency of this Japanese experience has encouraged hydrostructure in other parts of the world. Success is not immediate. Artificial reef building requires patience and a willingness to invest in the future. Apart from boat and tackle, today's fishermen make no investment in the ocean. The fish are there; man's investment is in the machinery necessary for the harvest.

Increasingly, to the dismay of fishermen and consumers paying exorbitant prices for food, the fish aren't there as they were. Fishermen run greater distances and are away longer to catch fewer fish.

Building and harvesting in the oceans do not occur contemporaneously. It requires about seven years for a lobster to grow to legal size, measuring 3 3/16 inches from the base of the eye socket to the end of carapace or body shell. Fish do not grow to consumable size overnight. Artificial reefs develop quickly, but like planting crops and raising animals on land, it requires an investment and time.

In the U.S., the State of Alabama was among the first to establish artificial offshore marine reefs. In 1953, Alabama Fish and Wildlife authorities placed 250 wrecked car bodies in the Gulf of Mexico. Within six months, fishermen reported catching snapper over these new "reefs." In 1957, Alabama sank 1500 more car bodies, reporting excellent fishing again after only six months on the bottom. The total cost for the project was $71,409, about $41 per car body, which Alabama officials felt was well spent in securing a return of recreational and commercial fishing to a previously barren area.

Many other states began to follow Alabama's lead. The Texas Parks and Wildlife Department has created underwater reefs with a variety of materials, including wrecked car bodies, concrete construction scrap, and imperfect roadway culverts.

In most of these experiments, it was found that car bodies and metal scrap were the least satisfactory building materials, corroding through the action of sea water. While crushed automobile bodies were effective for a short while and used to some advantage in the Gulf of Mexico, wildlife officials have preferred the use of imperfect concrete pipe, usually available free, culled from construction-damaged items or factory mismolds. Quarry stone is also an excellent base material.

A careful study was conducted in South Carolina by the Atlantic Estuarine Fisheries Center. Of some 114 approved artificial reefs on the Atlantic Coast of the U.S., approximately 43 of them contain about 600,000 scrap tires. To determine the effectiveness of this artificial reef building, a test location was chosen off Murrells Inlet, South Carolina. The area was surveyed before the test. It was found that there were only a few species of fish present. The invertebrate organisms that were present were found to be of little food value to the fish.

Scrap tires were sunk in the test area. The fisheries center reported that after about five months, barnacles that had first settled on the new artificial reef attained an average base diameter of 1/2 inch. After nine months many of the barnacles were grazed over by sea urchins and sheepshead. In the first nine-month period there had been a prolific growth of invertebrate organisms on the tire units, especially of sponges and hydroids. The fisheries center reported many small isopods, amphipods, and polychaete worms living in or on these animals.

Changing climatic conditions affected the cyclical growth and behavior of the organisms on the new reef. In short order, the marine community developed a clear food chain. The invertebrates became the prime food for fish. Black drum and sheepshead were abundant over the reef and on the average weighed from 2 to 4 pounds. In the cold months the sheepshead and drum were found living under the reef material, while sea trout schooled about and were seen feeding over the reefs. In the first year, as warmer weather approached again, crabs, black sea bass, pigfish, and pinfish were seen occupying the reef habitat, with an abundance of flounder and amberjack.

As a result of their studies, Atlantic Estuarine Fisheries Center scientists calculated that the overall fish-carrying capacity of the test area increased 300 to 1800 times.

Under the 1957 Dingell-Johnson Federal Aid in Fish Restoration Act, the U.S. Government has made aid available to the states for the construction of artificial reefs. Specific regulation vests in the U.S. Army Corps of Engineers under Section 10 of the 1899 River and Harbor Act, relating to obstruction or alteration of any navigable water of the U.S. The Outer Continental Shelf Lands Act of 1953 in Section 4 (f), specifically extends the Corps authority to artificial islands and offshore fixed structures. The U.S. Environmental Protection Agency regulates ocean dumping from a pollution standpoint and therefore must approve any intended reef-building project along with the Corps of Engineers.

Artificial reef building has become not only sanctioned in the U.S., but well regulated.

SHIPS AS TEACHERS

Shipwrecks, where most every available niche is overgrown with marine life, where the builders and producers are housed in self-contained underwater ecospheres, have laid the foundation for understanding the concepts involved in building artificial reefs.

The theory was nothing new, in fact nothing unexpected. Fishermen, from ancient times, have cast their nets perilously close to the location of underwater wrecks, knowing that that's where they'd find the largest catch.

In 1968, the State of Florida began a series of artificial reefs, sinking three ships in the Atlantic Ocean, about 3/4 mile off the Palm Beach Inlet. One of the ships was the Amaryllis, a 441-foot Greek freighter which had blown ashore on Singer Island during Hurricane Betsy. The other two consisted of the 185-foot antisubmarine escort, Mizpah, and a 165-foot patrol boat.

The ships were sunk in the Gulf Stream, where the current can attain 4 to 6 knots in velocity.

In short order these shipwrecks became havens for a wide variety of organisms. Huge jewfish inhabited their holds, reef fish cluttered their decks and superstructures, jacks, barracuda, and snapper cavorted among the sunken ships, seeking shelter from the swift current or food, eating the bountiful marine invertebrates growing on these artificial habitats, or the small fish attracted to them.

So successful were these initial reef building trials, that Florida upgraded the Palm Beach reefs in 1971, sinking a 65-foot tugboat, concrete rubble, and rubber tires. This foundation is today a fantastic underwater reef, providing habitable space and shelter where habitats were sparce in the swift Gulf Stream waters.

Common experience and the studies and observations of scientists and conservation officials of sunken warships and shipwrecks have led to the use of surplus Liberty ships from World War II for sinking as artificial reefs.

The idea occurred to Alabama state conservation officials who wished to take advantage of federal aid to states and a provision that would make these old ships available for sinking. On May 2, 1974, Alabama sank the first five of these old Liberty ships. In order to satisfy the Corps of Engineer permit requirements and preclude the possibility that the ships would become a hazard to navigation, they were stripped down and cut to a height of 15 feet, leaving a 416-foot-long by 50-foot-wide hull. The scrap value from the sale of the dismounted superstructures of the old Liberty ships paid for the cost of the artificial reef project.

The cut down hulks, weighing about 1,000 tons, were cleaned of oil and debris to meet EPA ocean-dumping standards and to avoid pollution of the water.

When all of the requirements were satisfied, Alabama officials towed the Liberty ships about 12 miles off Perdido Pass outside of Mobile Bay. The ships were sunk in about 85 feet of water by explosive charges placed by U.S. Navy demolition experts.

Alabama conservation officials report excellent fishing over the wrecks. Ling, dolphin, king mackerel, snapper, grouper and trigger-fish abound in an area which had been a sandy underwater desert. The artificial reefs have provided a refuge for smaller fish which attract the larger game fish.

Other Gulf Coast states have requested old Liberty ships for conversion into artificial reefs. On May 10, 1973, Texas applied for twelve of these Liberty ships from the Beaumont Defense Reserve for sinking in the Gulf of Mexico as authorized by the Texas Council on Marine Related Affairs.

In colder regions, such as the North Atlantic, although shipwrecks do not attract the magnificent and colorful array of coral abounding in tropical regions, the substrate serves in the same way to attract and house the invertebrate producers and builders. In short order the consumers appear on the scene and a viable productive underwater community blossoms. This is especially true on the shallower reaches of the Continental Shelf. A shallow plane extending as much as 200 miles out to sea, the Atlantic Continental Shelf gradually slopes off. It is not uncommon off the Atlantic coast, to find shipwrecks some 20 miles at sea, in only about 80 feet of water. Around the shipwreck, life abounds. Ocean pouts sulk in the debris, ling parade over the decks, starfish and anemone adhere to the iron plates while lobster crouch in the deep recesses, sponges adorn the hull. These old ships, some torpedoed by German U-boats during the war, others claimed by marine disaster, play host to a variety of cold-water marine life.

These shipwrecks are like great blossoming oases in the middle of the desert. Around them, the sandy bottom is barren, fairly empty of life, unable to support life because of the lack of suitable habitats that provide attachable surfaces. In the midst of these barren sandy reaches, sunken ships become veritable masterpieces of creation, proving that no habitable space in nature is ever wasted.

Six months after the sinking of the coastwise tanker, the *Chester A. Poling*, in the Atlantic just off Gloucester Harbor, I observed attaching organisms beginning to take hold on her deck and structures.

Fish were moving comfortably over the wreck, beginning to pick at the invertebrate organisms that already settled on her hull. In eight months, the valves and pipes were converted into flowering life. Nature was beginning to convert the wreck into a center for life under the sea.

While it is far too early to draw any scientific conclusions about the growth of marine organisms on recently sunk ships like the *Poling,* significant insight about the use of shipwrecks as substrate for artificial underwater reefs has been gathered as an unintended side effect of World War II.

The greatest laboratory in the world for the study of substrate growth lies at the bottom of Truk Lagoon in Micronesia. It is at the same time a unique marine phenomenon and a great adventure into the underwater realm. The product of a violent battle, Truk is also a legacy of war. The history of Truk, the formation and growth of Truk's majestic coral gardens, the wonderment of life inhabiting the sunken

A steering wheel protrudes from one of the vehicles stowed as deck cargo on one of the large Japanese freighters. The ship was sunk during the first day's Allied air attack on Truk's anchorage. Since the ship went down in February 1944, scientists have a substrate of known origin enabling them to measure coral and the development of marine life. Algae and colorful sponges overgrow the wheel, while hard brain coral clumps are visible growing on the ship's steel-plated deck.

ships, provide a scientific time capsule for the study of how hydrostructure can be expected to work. Truk is a diver's fantasy and, as we will see, science's Paradise Lost, found.

There is an indescribable thrill of discovery while swimming inside these shipwrecks. It is somewhat akin to finding a city, long forgotten, under the sea. They are immense, like cities, these great vessels with holds and hatchways so vast that squadrons of fighter planes still lie nested in their cargo spaces, stacked symmetrically; an air force that never flew. There are war vehicles stowed below the decks of freighters; brand new fleets of trucks that never drove over land, cargo aboard some sixty ships of all description, ships that never sail. The largest navy in the world was discovered a few yards at a time, twenty fathoms under the sea.

Long dark corridors are patrolled by fish, guns are silhouetted against a cyan sea, and catwalks and bridges are overgrown with coral. Clothed in so many garlands of color, it is hard to imagine that war had any part of this; so silent are the warships, bathed in calm.

Truk had become Japan's Gibralter of the Pacific, hardly a welcome role for these sleepy Eastern Caroline Islands located in the mid-Pacific, some 565 nautical miles southeast of Guam, 3075 nautical miles southwest of Hawaii, lying 1842 nautical miles east-south-east of Tokyo. It was a role suggested by Truk's strategic advantage and the sheltered lagoon, deep enough for the largest warships to anchor inside the protected safety of a natural fringing reef.

Historically the islands in Micronesia had been occupied by Spain in the eighteenth century. After the Spanish-American War, Germany seized control of the islands. Japanese expeditionary forces pushed the Germans out during World War I. The Japanese Imperial Navy occupied the German territories of the Caroline, Mariana, and Marshall Islands. Fighting on the side of the Allies during the First World War, Japan negotiated a treaty with Great Britain, France, and Russia, which granted Japan sovereign ownership of Micronesia after the war. At the close of hostilities, however, Japan was given only a mandate by the League of Nations to administer Micronesia.

Secretly, Japan violated Article IV of the League's mandate, wherein Japan had agreed that "no military or naval bases shall be established or fortifications erected" in Micronesia. The fortifications, replete with underground tunnels and well-armed cement bunkers and defensive bulwarks, were amazing logistical feats considering they were constructed clandestinely over a period of years.

Truk was made the main headquarters command for Japan's Fourth Fleet. Warships entered Truk on December 10, 1939. Detailed to the Japanese Fleet Command were squadrons of seaplanes and Mavis flying boats.

On February 16, 1944, the first wave of 72 American fighter planes was launched from aircraft carriers in the American task force that included sixteen battleships and cruisers.

Navy pilots shot down Japanese planes over Truk in the air and on the airfields of Moen, Eten, and Param Islands inside the lagoon. U.S. Navy reports tallied 260 Japanese planes destroyed on the first day. Just before dawn on February 17, 1944, the American planes returned loaded with 369 thousand-pound bombs, 498 five-hundred-pound bombs and 76 torpedoes. In all, the carrier task force launched thirty waves of continuous attack planes against Japanese shipping on the second day of fighting.

American submarines coordinated their attack to catch Japanese shipping trying to flee the lagoon. The Naval Task Force under Admiral Spruance sunk the Japanese cruiser *Katori*, the destroyer *Maikaze* and trawler *Shonan* as they tried to flee through Truk's North Pass through the reef. Only one ship, the destroyer *Nowaki*, escaped.

At the end of the two days fighting, more than 200,000 tons of Japanese shipping lay on the bottom of Truk Lagoon. The toll included fifteen Japanese naval ships, seventeen cargo ships and six tankers. Destroyed in the fighting were more than 275 Japanese and American planes, many of them plummeting into the lagoon.

The main fighting force of the Japanese fleet abandoned Truk after the February onslaught, but shipping continued to use the anchorage and resupply the land forces on Truk. On April 29 and 30, 1944, and again in May and June of that year, additional air attacks on Truk chalked up more sinkings, bringing the toll of vessels on the bottom of the lagoon to about 65. Eventually, American pressure on the Marianas and their fall in July, 1944, made reinforcement of Truk impossible.

The ground war passed Truk by. After destroying the islands effectiveness as an air base and sinking a major segment of the Japanese fleet, U.S. military strategists decided to by-pass Truk in favor of capturing islands closer to Japan that could be used as bases for the B-29 bombers.

Japanese Vice-Admiral Chuicki Hara and Lieutenant General Shurzabura Magikura surrendered Truk on September 2, 1945, to

83

U.S. Navy Vice-Admiral George D. Murray, aboard the flagship Portland.

For the eleven larger islands and dozens of little islets inside Truk's 40-mile-wide lagoon, the war was over. Scarred and torn by the violence, these small volcanic isles were left to settle with the chaos remaining after the destruction. The Trukese came out of hiding in their caves and slowly they regained their obscurity and remote unimportance as a sleepy peacefulness returned to Micronesia.

No one bothered with the shipwrecks, at least not in any appreciable way. Scuba diving was in its infancy after the war and there was no general access to the equipment. The Trukese had little interest in the wrecks since the remoteness of the islands made salvage impractical, and there were no markets for the artifacts. Nature took her course. The tropical foliage reclaimed the land cleared for airstrips, fast overgrowing the concrete bunkers and gun emplacements. Underwater, the first attaching organisms began to grow on the substrate of sunken ships.

As the shipwrecks in Truk settled, after the oil, aviation fuel, and toxic debris had done its harm and been washed out to sea, nature's creatures began to investigate these huge iron derelicts and slowly, though unseen and unstudied, the first vestiges of life began to sprout on and inside them. Ample tenants took up residence in this new underwater housing development. Creatures began to seek refuge in these sunken ships, setting up their lives in a complex interdependent chain of plant and animal producers and consumers.

The steel behemoths of Truk Lagoon have provided the substrate for a variety of attaching organisms. Coral and sponges are abundant as are sea anemone and algae. Schools of small silver baitfish dart about the wrecks while large groupers prowl the holds and companionways and sharks take up solemn convoy duty alongside the doomed ships.

My friend Kimiuo Aisek, who was just seventeen when the attack on Truk began, now owns a small dive shop on Moen Island. Kimiuo is philosophical about the events that molded an important part of world history. He remembers the Japanese who pressed Trukese into labor parties. He has seen the shipwrecks develop from barren oil- and gas-exuding monsters to placid flower gardens. Kimiuo told me that it required more than two years for the major oil spills from ruptured Japanese tankers to dissipate.

"There is still some danger from the bombs. Most of the oil has stopped leaking and the lagoon has been healed," Kimiuo said, one afternoon as his wife prepared us a meal of fish, speared in front of his dive shop, cooked in coconut milk.

Kimiuo has tried to forget the war. His interest now is in showing the few dive visitors to Truk the beauty that has taken over the wrecks.

As we dove over the sunken ships, my Trukese friends would point out the majestic coral. It was often impossible to recognize the underlying substrate, so ornately had nature applied its cosmetic.

Clearly, from afar, the outline of a ship's cannon was ominous, looming up from the deck. Dominating the panorama, a huge Stylophora coral almost 6 feet across sat perched on the gun. Hundreds of gaily colored fish darted in and out of the coral. The gun's breach was engraved with sponges, algae, and smaller coral growths. Perhaps a dozen varieties were crammed together, sharing the gears and firing mechanisms, until all that was visible was a panorama of color.

Wires and chains, railings and deck fittings were all overgrown with life. Even the bombs, mines, depth charges and bullets were decorated with living organisms. Unknowing creatures perched with aplomb upon the massive 18-inch shells inside the cargo hold of the ammunition ship *Yamagiri Maru*. Each of these 18-inch-diameter projectiles for the largest naval cannons ever made cost the price of a Cadillac automobile to manufacture. Each was capable of being fired 20 miles from the special naval guns of the Japanese battleships *Yamato* and *Mushashi*, among the largest dreadnaughts ever built. It didn't seem to matter that these massive bombs and projectiles were still capable of great destruction; the projectiles were encrusted with life.

Decks and cowlings festooned with coral, brightly ornate and colorful soft coral, hard brain coral, and fingers of dozens of varieties of madrepore graced the metal protrusions.

In Truk's reef environment there is a close interdependence between the marine algae, the coral, and fish. Clumps of green Halimeda algae overgrew the shipwrecks, and beautiful symmetric clumps of grapelike Caulerpa algae hung precariously from the bridges and brasswork.

Marine plants form the basis of a tropical reef community, attaching willy-nilly to substrate where sunlight can penetrate the sea. Fish are at the other end of the complex interrelating chain of life, feeding on the plants, on coral, and on other fish or small marine animals attracted to the reef.

Careful study has and will enable scientists to better understand the phenomena of coral growth and the ecological relationships of creatures on a reef community of dated origin. Starting with February,

1944, scientists know that no growth could have taken place prior to the ships going down. Careful measurements of coral, divided by the maximum number of years under the sea, have given evidence for example, that the Stylophora coral grows at the rate of about 2 inches a year.

The underwater environment in Truk is full of startling surprises. Even though the events surrounding the bombing attacks on Truk are modern history, already many mysteries have puzzled explorers and scientists still seeking to find and identify some of the sunken ships and learn about their ill-fated crews.

Tragic accidents have added to the lore of Truk. The Japanese had five submarines anchored off Dublon Island. Warned of attacking B-29 aircraft, the U-boats submerged. The ventilating tube on one of the submarines, the I-169, was left open or it jammed. As a result, the 330-foot I class vessel flooded and sank. With her seventy-seven-man crew still trapped inside, the Japanese vainly attempted to salvage her. Failing in their attempts, they finally depth charged the U-boat themselves to prevent it from falling into allied hands.

I had to receive special permission to dive with my companions on the I-169. The Truk government placed the submarine off limits after a diver became trapped inside the sub and lost his life. The vessel is in about 140 feet of water.

Swimming down the anchor line, the hulk of the I-169 became visible on the bottom when we reached about 90 feet. The long sleek lines of the U-boat are unmistakable. The sub is intact from the engine room to the after torpedo compartment and propellers. Long strands of wire coral twist their narrow fingers 30 or 40 feet up from the deck. Schools of fish prowl the perforated gratings over the sub's pressure hull. The eerie stillness and sense of depth adds to the impression of doom as one swims over the U-boat.

Even the hatches of the I-169 are covered with life. Nature has covered the tomb with a wreath of beauty and color.

In a rare ceremony, relatives of the long dead crewmen of the I-169, returned to Truk many years later. In a memorial service, they paid their respects to the dead, taking the skeleton remains of the trapped seamen back to Japan for burial.

There are many oddities, clearly reminiscent of those horrible days of 1944, scattered on the lagoon floor. I didn't recognize them at first, covered as they were with such diverse sea life: umbrellas of coral, large rooster comb oysters, *Tridacna maxima,* giant clams, and prongs of staghorn coral. Seeing these torpedoes, unexploded and still filled with their charges of high explosive, swimming close to them and feeling their iron sides, one gets a clear impression of their potential violence and power. With a fearless abandon, nature has built fine sponge and coral lattice work, tempering their awesome power. Each torpedo represents an artificial reef community, complete, interwoven, with each creature in residence vying and defending his place on the bomb, his right to live, his centimeter on the warhead, where not just life, but a living community has been created. The sunken planes have been turned into forests, their cockpits overgrown with plants. The machine guns are painted pink with sponges. Compasses, brown and green with algae, still bear true, on a course heading nowhere.

Swimming through the fuselage and into the cockpit of a sunken four engine *Kawanishi* T-97 seaplane, the same panoply of color and life sprouts from every surface. Glass is still intact in the cockpit, controls grown over with coral, glazed with bright colors. In one of the sunken planes, a panel of instruments survived the crash and the oil-filled gauges are still intact. I rubbed the glass with my finger, removing the growth. The instruments were still functional.

In the holds of the 436-foot aircraft ferry *Fujikawa Maru*, a cargo of new Zero fighter planes lie just as they were stowed. Squeezing into the pilot's seat, one can touch the controls, imagining the battle, pushing the curious fish away as they poke at the bubbles leaving the dive regulator.

In the cargo spaces of the 350-foot *Sankisan Maru*, new trucks are stowed with cases of ammunition. New war materiel, finally put in service a hundred feet below the surface, is used by colorful soldier fish, playing between the steering column and gear shift.

There are sobering reminders about these silent warriors. Inside the crew's quarters, effects of sailors are still in place on their shelves, silted over, stacked as they were left, tennis shoes, gas masks, shaving equipment, and personal property, grim reminders that men died here. It is inevitable that we would find them; there were thousands after all.

There, amid the wreckage, amid the hulks overgrown with life, the skeletons of Japanese sailors, skulls and bones settled in the silt, proof positive of the anomaly, the unnatural case of man and nature.

Truk had been left behind by time, only occasionally visited by the scientist or adventurous sport diver. There had been a short-lived interest in the munitions in the wrecks, when an enterprising, but illegal, fishing consortium was put together. The Trukese entrepreneurs would dive down and recover live bombs which they would bring to the surface, saw in half, extracting the explosive powder. This explosive would then be placed in smaller bombs and used to dynamite fish the reefs. This almost clandestine operation would have become a thriving enterprise except for the fact that one of the hapless entrepreneurs insisted on smoking on the job. In a moment of carelessness, he flicked a cigarette into the live powder, suddenly and sensationally ending the business venture.

A law now makes it illegal for anyone to disturb these shipwrecks or to remove artifacts from them. Until recently, Truk was governed by the United States under a UN Trusteeship, and a High Commissioner for Micronesia, appointed by the President, officiated at the seat of government in Saipan, 590 nautical miles from Truk Lagoon. Autonomy and self government have recently been granted to the island states that make up Micronesia, although each island state remains federated to and represented by the United States for matters such as defense and foreign affairs.

At least for now, Truk's unique marine laboratory, its undersea research center for the study of nature's creative process, will remain unspoiled for future study.

STUDYING SHIPWRECKS

The study of war relics and shipwrecks, such as those on the bottom of Truk lagoon, provide ample evidence of the efficacy of artificial reefs. Truk lagoon remains a magnificently equipped biological center for study of the effects of substrate growth, animal behavior and relationships which are required for a viable marine ecosystem to exist.

Of course these shipwrecks may disintegrate in time, finally collapsing into the sea. Eventually, perhaps in another fifty years, the magnificent coral gardens in Truk lagoon may crumble into obscure heaps on the sandy bottom. Even though they are temporary, we have learned from these shipwrecks the value of building in the sea, of creating habitats that will support life. Underwater habitats will expand the ocean's ability to support life where little or none existed before. We are learning the principles of converting barron sandy reaches in the ocean, on the Continental Shelf, in the Gulf of Mexico, or places like Truk lagoon into productive life-sustaining and food-producing environments. With these foundations, responsible public officials have begun experiments to determine the feasibility of constructing artificial reefs to serve as fishhavens. Scientists have begun undertaking the experiments that will eventually lead to choice materials and techniques, ever perfecting this inexact process I have named hydrostructure.

The ability of the sea to produce food for ever increasing populations may provide the key to man's continued survival. It is perhaps ironic that the horror of war has left us this legacy of life. Sunken ships, torpedoed and bombed to oblivion, have become memorialized by this beauty under the sea. They have shown us a way of creating and sustaining life that may someday avert a more horrible war where people fight over dwindling food resources.

Already governments are taking forward-thinking steps to sink surplus Liberty ships as foundations for underwater reefs, while scientists continue to seek ways to perfect their understanding of what we have thus far learned from the study of wrecks underwater for known periods of time. War has left us the legacy of Truk lagoon. I hope we will reinvest this inheritance into a system of planting in the sea in order that we may reap dividends for a better tomorrow.

7

Man's Intrusion

TREASURE AND HISTORY

They are a breed apart, adventurers with romantic notions of discovery, soldiers of fortune. Some treasure divers are scoundrels turned marine archaeologists, some do not bother to hide the fact that they are just plain rogues, and some are just businessmen who poke around shipwrecks on week-ends, hoping to make a find. Whatever their category, divers have been tempted for centuries by the lure of discovering gold underwater.

New inventions, technological advances in the underwater treasure hunter's field equipment, have converted the sea-going panhandler into a rather sophisticated technician. Treasure salvors have recruited scientists with side scan sonar, magnetometers, and a variety of midget submarines to aid them in their quest for riches under the sea.

Some of the most important discoveries of underwater caches of gold or important historic artifacts have been made after careful research led underwater explorers to the site of a marine tragedy. Earthquakes or volcanoes, hurricanes, tempests, and war have sunk untold numbers of ships, even pushed whole cities and civilizations into the sea. Once submerged, this wreckage becomes part of the underwater environment, fast converted into usable living space by a variety of marine organisms.

In 1902, Saint-Pierre was a bustling metropolis. Architecturally, intellectually, culturally, the city was the center of colonial life on the island of Martinique and the administrative capital of the French West Indies. That was before eight o'clock on the morning of May 8, 1902. At two minutes after eight, the entire city was engulfed in flames, its 30,000 inhabitants annihilated, the fourteen ships riding at anchor in the Bay of Saint-Pierre sunk.

The very few who survived the tragic aftermath of the eruption of Mont Pelée described the black cloud of fire and death which descended on them as the searing volcanic explosions spewed burning ash over the entire city.

The French commander of *Le Suchet*, a naval cruiser on station in Martinique, sailed his ship into Saint-Pierre Bay shortly after the eruption. Commander Le Bris' cable to the French Naval Ministry described what he saw: "Returned from Saint-Pierre. City completely destroyed by mass of fire eight o'clock this morning. Suppose entire population annihilated; brought back the few survivors, thirty people. All ships at anchorage burned and lost; I leave for Guadeloupe, the volcano continues to erupt."

Not since the eruption of Mount Vesuvius destroyed the cities of Pompeii and Herculaneum in 79 A.D., some two thousand years before, had a volcano erupted with such force or taken such a tragic toll of lives. Researching the maritime aspects of this disaster in the Vulcanological Museum in Saint-Pierre, I came across macabre documentary photographs depicting curious visitors, after the eruption, walking among grotesque cadavers of the victims' incinerated remains. Some of the curious posed with the cadavers, bodies frozen in death, solidified as if carved out of stone where and as they fell, instantly killed and mummified by the searing heat.

The maritime disaster was chronicled by Alfred LaCroix, a volcanologist dispatched from France to study the tragedy and take depositions from the survivors. A few of the sailors fared better than the city dwellers. All save one of the ships sank at anchor in the bay. A handful of sailors aboard the *Roddam* managed to upanchor and make for the island of Saint Lucia, sustaining heavy damage and casualties.

LaCroix interviewed the second officer of the sailing ship *Gabrielle*, Georges Marie Sainte. The officer watched from deck as Mont Pelée erupted. He saw the enveloping cloud of burning ash descend over the city. Sainte was saved, for when the explosive volcanic force reached his ship and she was dismasted and violently thrown over on her side, the vessel remained afloat for a short while, supported by the buoyancy of her empty cargo holds.

When I explored the *Gabrielle* underwater, I found that the vessel lay flat out in the sand. There was extensive deterioration to the hull of the wooden merchant sailing ship. It was clear from the artifacts we discovered, ship's china and fittings, that she had been finely appointed. In 1902, the *Gabrielle* belonged to the Knight mercantile establishment which, at the turn of the century, operated a major warehouse and store in the city of Saint-Pierre, prospering from their West Indies trade.

The wreck of the *Gabrielle* was discovered at a depth of 36 meters, almost 1 kilometer offshore, directly in front of what is now Saint-Pierre's new cement pier. The hull which remained protruding from the sand was overgrown with sponges, soft coral, black wire coral, and anemone.

One of the vessels sunk by the volcano was the huge Quebec liner *Roraima*. The *Roraima*, a metal-hulled steamship, was the largest of the vessels at anchor in the Bay. Her cargo was combustible potassium. It ignited and the huge ship burned furiously for three days before going under.

The *Roraima* was sunk in deep water, limiting access to divers without submitting themselves to long decompression. Her metal hulk lies in from 50 to 64 meters, upright in the sand, listing to port.

Swimming over the wreck, we found it relatively intact except for the bow, which had separated from the main section of the ship. The huge wreck provides a majestic underwater spectacle. Her decks, promenades, companionways, and superstructure are overgrown with long spindly strands of black wire coral and small black coral trees. Garlands of sponge and anemone grow over the rusting metal plates. Fish range in and out of the cargo holds and cabins.

The diver's atmosphere is heavy at the *Roraima's* depth. The sounds from the regulator reverberate with a faraway dullness. Lightheadedness, the effect of nitrogen narcosis, adds to the sullen spectacle of the wreck.

Ladders overgrown with wire coral extend into cavernous holds leading deep inside the bowels of the *Roraima*. Years of silt have accumulated on the ship's walkways inside the hold, blanketing railings and cargo decks. Brass vacuum-tube lamps grace her internal compartments, fixed to the ship's bulkheads. She was a steamship and generated electricity from her steam boiler.

Jutting masts and hoists, wires brown with rust and silt protrude upward from the ship's deck, overgrown with coral and marine life.

The *Roraima* is an eerie ship, deep and dark, massive in the stillness of the Bay.

The *Roraima's* sister ship, the Quebec liner *Roddam*, had just arrived in Saint-Pierre Bay at 6:45 on the morning of May 8, 1902. The crew of the *Roddam* had barely set her anchor when Mont Pelée exploded. Luckily the crew of the *Roddam* was on deck and alert. The *Roddam* caught fire but was not completely destroyed by the sudden fury of the eruption. The *Roddam's* captain, E.W. Freeman's account of the tragedy remains one of the most graphic, reported by LaCroix in his chronicle. Captain Freeman's eyewitness report of the events was made in the following terms: "All of a sudden there was a violent detonation that shook the land and the sea. There was a formidable explosion of the mountain from the summit to its base, giving rise to a flashing flame, lanced into the air, followed by a tremendous force of immense black clouds. These clouds enveloped the mountain and descended like a cyclone bounding over all obstacles. Then, when the clouds reached the city, plunging it into darkness they headed toward the ships anchored in the bay. The clouds of cinders and searing hot air reached the water, its massive force hurtling against the ships. The *Roraima* was pushed over on its side, the *Roddam* half-submerged. The *Grappler* sank immediately."

Other shipwrecks now on the bottom of Saint-Pierre Bay provided us with graphic insight into life and activities in the bustling port city of Saint-Pierre in 1902. One sailing merchant ship, the *Teresa Lovico*, was loaded with a cargo of building materials. Tiles and cement in barrels, coiled manila rope, remain stacked on deck in much the same way they were originally stowed. The cement hardened, taking the shape of the barrels, standing upright on the *Lovico's* rotted deck, gaunt memorials to the sailors who lost their lives aboard the ship.

As we fanned some of the silt and debris with our hands aft, in a section that apparently served as the galley, we unearthed human skeletal remains, mute testimony of the tragedy that befell the officers and crew of the *Lovico*. We disturbed the human remains as little as possible, removing some of them out of the silt and sand we had stirred up to document them on film, putting the bones back where they had been when we were through.

The old vessel was brass and copper fastened. Her planking joined with hand-wrought spikes and nails. Hand-blown bottles gave us some clues about how the wreck was provisioned. Even the hand-blown bottles we recovered were covered with sponges and marine algae.

Early photographs of the anchorage of Saint-Pierre showed the fourteen ships lined up fore and aft, perpendicular to the shore, prows facing out to sea. Seeing the disarray of the wreckage underwater, realizing these huge ocean-going ships were tossed about like so many matchboxes by the fury of the eruption, gives credence to the story of the mechanic aboard the *Teresa Lovico*, who survived the event to recount his version of the sinking.

The *Lovico*, according to her mechanic Jean Louis, was moored at the foot of Rue d'Orange at the southern end of the city, some 50 meters from shore. Jean Louis reported that there had been a huge welling up of the sea at about 11 o'clock on the night of May 7. At seven o'clock the next morning, Jean Louis reported seeing a jet of steam vapor emanate from the volcano. At eight as Jean Louis described: "An enormous mass of the crater detached and was hurled toward the city. In a moment I lost consciousness, was thrown down where I was standing, bodies of my comrades fell on top of me. I came to, the houses in the city were on fire, the rum factories were exploding one after another, the trees were leafless, but were not burning." Jean Louis abandoned his sinking ship by jumping into the sea, eventually being rescued by the French cruiser *Le Suchet*.

The horror of this disaster can be understood from Captain Freeman's account of the *Roddam's* escape. He reported: "The sea was rough. We navigated blindly for five hours. It seemed we crossed a great obscurity in our escape. At five o'clock in the evening we made the island of Saint Lucia. Our decks were covered with cinders. The wounded were finally taken off to hospitals. Many had died. In the days that followed, we were given permission to clear the ship of debris. It required three days for the ash to sufficiently cool before it could be removed. Layers of ash and cinders covered our decks. Workers removed 120 tons of ash; I can give that figure exactly, because we were not authorized to dump the material in the port, rather it had to be discharged into a barge that held 20 tons. The barge hauled away six full loads of cinders from the *Roddam's* decks. The ship was in a pitiful state. Only her hull and machinery remained."

From the reports of Captain Freeman recorded at the time and others, our exploration of these shipwrecks took on historical perspective. The eruption of Mont Pelée was not only a human but an environmental disaster.

These shipwrecks, like those described in Truk Lagoon, provide a historic site for the study of nautical archaeology, and a time capsule for anthropologists. Naturalists, as long as these old wooden wrecks hold their shape and structure, will be able to use Saint-Pierre Bay as a laboratory for the study of West Indies coral and marine life. Martinique fishermen with less intricate purposes, continue to cast their nets perilously close to the old wrecks, harvesting a good day's catch around them. Whatever the historic value of these old ships, there is a natural advantage to the ecological community, a fishing village depends on the results of this tragic event for subsistence. A by-product of the tragedy of Mont Pelée's eruption was the creation in Saint-Pierre Bay of one of the underwater marvels of the world.

SPANISH TREASURE GALLEONS

With a cargo valued at over $100 million, the *Nuestra Señora de Atocha* sank in 1622 off the Florida Keys. More than 40 tons of treasure, including gold and silver, sank with her.

They recovered 901 silver bars, 161 discs of gold and 265,000 silver coins from the wreck of the *Atocha*. The salvage was not without great sacrifice and personal tragedy for treasure hunter Mel Fisher who discovered the wreck after years of plodding research in the Archivo General de los Indes in Seville, Spain.

In the spring of 1973, Mel Fisher outfitted the *Southwind*, a square, top heavy tugboat, as the base of operations for his company, Treasure Salvors, Inc. While on the treasure site, the tug took water in her bilges and capsized. Mel's son Dirk, Dirk's wife and Rick Gage, who had been asleep in their bunks, lost their lives in the accident.

The *Atocha's* treasure was finally salvaged by Fisher's company under license from the state of Florida. The *Atocha's* astrolabe, one of the few remaining navigational instruments of this type in the world, was found by Dirk Fisher before his death and remains one of the most important underwater artifacts discovered.

Many important underwater discoveries have been found, not by accident or advanced science-fiction-like technology, but by the dogged persistence of ordinary men who have come upon their finds after years of searching.

One of the first to discover the remains of the Spanish Plate Fleet, sunk in a hurricane off the Florida Keys on July 15, 1733, was Art McKee. Art had been employed in Florida as a hard-hat diver, installing and repairing pilings for bridges and causeways connecting the Keys. As a form of relaxation, McKee took to diving on the reefs. In 1948, McKee made his first finds of ballast stones and ship's cannon. Among his early discoveries were some silver coins bearing the 1732 Mexico City mintmark.

What McKee had stumbled on were the remains of the greatest treasure fleet ever assembled. The ships of the 1733 Plate Fleet were carrying back to Spain the annual output of the mint at Mexico City, along with a king's ransom of treasures brought across the Pacific from Spain's far flung possessions in the Philippines and her lucrative China trade. These treasures had been accumulated at Acapulco and carried overland to Vera Cruz on the backs of Indian slaves to be put aboard the treasure fleet sailing home to Spain.

After his initial finds in 1948, Art McKee labored for more than eleven years in the waters off Vaca Key, excavating the remains of the 1733 Plate Fleet. In addition to a wealth of ingots of gold and silver, coins and jewels, thousands of artifacts from the ships themselves, including ornaments, ship's utensils and accouterments as well as personal possessions from the passengers and crew, made the McKee treasure finds the most important discovered in the Americas up to that time.

McKee and his divers found examples of early Chinese porcelain. Magnificent examples of Chinese craftsmanship that survived the ardors of a perilous voyage across the Pacific, thence by land through treacherous mountain passes from Acapulco, to the cabins of Don Rodrigo de Torres' ships, massing up stores of wealth of the New World for the trip back to Spain.

McKee found uniform buckles, buttons, insignia and military equipment encrusted among the coral. At first blush, they appeared as unrecognizable masses of the bottom, fused with the living reef. In the more than two centuries since the treasure fleet sank off Vaca Key, crushed upon the coral reef by the fury of a sudden storm, nature had worked its miracle and almost completely consumed and covered the wreckage.

Imbedded in the coral masses, McKee found human teeth and animal bones in a remarkable state of preservation. Dirks and swords, flintlock pistols and rifles were recovered from the wreck sites, embellished with an array of coral and marine growth. Without a keen eye, a diver would have completely overlooked these relics. They resembled the coral that had long ago set up residence around the artifact, disguising it as an integral part of the living reef.

McKee had X-rays taken of some of these encrusted masses so that they could break them apart without damaging delicate pieces inside the thick coral crusts. In one of these X-ray pictures, the distinct outline of a flintlock pistol was visible with a lead ball in the breech, indicating that the pistol was charged and ready. While history makes no mention of the fate of the sailor who last held the pistol or charged it to defend his ship's cargo of treasure against the uncertainties of the voyage, the natural forces that dashed his ship on the reef had also, in time, enveloped his pistol in a mantle of coral.

Personal effects recovered by Art McKee provided some insight into life aboard ship in the New World. Wooden lemon juice squeezers indicated that the crew took on stores of the citrus fruit to stave off the dreaded scurvy which always claimed the lives of sailors on the long voyages from home who were forced to eat rations devoid of proper nutrients. Clay smoking pipes, medicine and liquor bottles and food jars with remnants of their original contents intact, gave historians some insight into the habits of these early Spanish Conquistadores.

Art McKee left many of the artifacts in their original state, just as he recovered them underwater, thick encrustations intact. Pieces of sail cloth, hemp, stitching needles and morsels of ship's rigging were found amazingly preserved, converted by nature into a substrate for the reef.

Eighteen ships of Don Rodrigo's ill-fated convoy were sunk off Florida's coast as they navigated perilously close to shore. Some of McKee's most surprising finds included primitive navigational instruments. A wooden sextant, recovered intact, was recognizable under its cloak of coral. With some of the encrustations chipped away, one carefully restored segment of the bare wood of a sextant still bears minute calibrations used to calculate the ship's position.

One of McKee's most unusual discoveries came when they broke apart two cannon from the sixty-gun British man-of-war, *H.M.S. Winchester*, which sank off Carysfort Reef in the Florida Keys. The *Winchester* was returning to England in 1695 from convoy duty in Jamaica. Most of the crew were sick or dying from scurvy when the ship hit a reef and foundered helplessly.

When McKee found the shipwreck, he saw two cannon crossed underwater. They were cemented together by years of coral growth. When the cannon were brought to the surface and eventually broken apart, the divers found a seaman's prayer book. The pages were preserved and protected from the action of the sea water by the weight of the cannon and the subsequent coral encrustations.

McKee's observations and the encrusted artifacts give some insight into the way marine organisms establish habitats on a reef. It was the impetus for gold and treasure that brought discovery to the New World. Hundreds of years later, it was that same lure of gold and discovery that renewed interest in the exploration of Florida's underwater reefs.

A natural disaster accounted for one of the most unusual underwater excavations in North America. Used as a retreat for pirates, the Jamaican city of Port Royal became a British fortress after the capture of the island in 1655. Privateers used Port Royal to attack Spanish shipping in the Caribbean. On June 7, 1692, a violent earthquake shook the peninsula and pushed nine-tenths of the city into the sea. Two thousand of the city's eight thousand inhabitants lost their lives in the earthquake and another thousand perished in the epidemics that followed the tragedy.

Port Royal lay submerged under silt and mud for more than two and a half centuries until Ed Link and later Bob Marx began excavating the ruins in the bay.

Over eighteen hundred buildings including five entire forts were swept into the sea in a three-square-mile area. Bob Marx's excavation of Port Royal required three years. During that time they brought up 900,000 bricks, the remains from a total of 600 human beings, 4 tons of animal bones and some 12,000 intact clay pipes, the bowls of 50,000 others, some with their tobacco wads still intact. Marx and his divers recovered 26,000 antique onion bottles as well as almost a million iron artifacts.

The first coins Marx found underwater in the submerged city of Port Royal were counterfeits. They were copper planchets covered with what was at the time considered a worthless metal, platinum. Marx found weights and scales underwater bearing the hallmarks of 1692's equivalent of the Inspector of Weights and Measures. The weights tested short, indicating that the early inhabitants of Port Royal were taken over by the same kind of consumer fraud which has, alas, carried over into modern times. The divers also discovered many valuable coins and jewels and an assortment of relics of life in early Jamaica.

Of particular interest were a series of turtle crawls located in one area of what was Fisher's Row. In the crawls Marx and his divers recovered a large quantity of sea turtle bones. It appeared that the inhabitants of Port Royal trapped the turtles and kept them in the crawls until they were ready to use them for food. Remnants of meals left in kitchen utensils showed that turtle stew was a popular dish in old Port Royal.

One of Bob Marx's most famous discoveries was that of the treasure galleon *Nuestra Señora de las Maravillas,* sunk in 1656 about 40 miles northeast of the Bahamas North Bank. In the first week after his discovery, Marx had recovered two buckets full of uncut emeralds, 260 tons of silver in bars, 300 chests of jewels, 58 bronze cannon, quantities of coins and valuable artifacts that stagger the imagination.

Marx had searched twelve years for the *Maravilla* until finally in 1972 he found the shipwreck directly under an old iron vessel that had subsequently wrecked in the same spot.

Another of those legendary New World shipwrecks was recently discovered in an area called the Silver Shoals. In early times the island of Santo Domingo was known as Hispaniola and the Silver Shoals nicknamed Ambrosia Banks. In 1659, *Nuestra Señora de la Concepción* was caught in a raging storm and wrecked on a shallow reef.

A *flota* of thirty ships including the *Nuestra Señora de la Concepción* set sail from Havana for Spain on September 13, 1659. The *Concepción* was leaking and in need of repairs. A day and a half after the treasure fleet left Havana, they were forced to put back to shore in order that divers could repair the *Concepción's* rotting timbers. The ship was taking water.

The *flota* put back out to sea but was caught by the full gale force of a hurricane in the Florida Straits. The *Concepción* remained afloat. Dismasted and leaking badly, the crew tried to sail her for Puerto Rico. After a week's foundering, the *Concepción* drifted into dangerous shoals where coral reefs were visible breaking near the surface.

Her crew worked valiantly to tow the treasure galleon through the reefs, rowing the long boats in front of her. The crew had thrown over the vessel's cannon for anchor, the ship having lost her regular anchor in the storm. One night this jury rigged anchor line parted and the *Concepción* crashed against the reef. The ship swung around and was buffeted against the coral, ripping open the hull, spilling her precious cargo over the reef.

Only 190 of the 514 members of the Spanish crew escaped the wreck. They took with them as many chests of treasure as they could carry off the doomed ship. Spain, at war with privateers commissioned by England and France, never salvaged the *Concepción.* Years later in 1683, King Charles II of England set two vessels out to find the *Concepción,* neither succeeded.

An American adventurer, William Phips, convinced King Charles that he could succeed where the two other captains failed. Phips was commissioned with a small ship, the *Rose Algier* and ninety men. After near mutiny and two years of bad luck, Phips came upon a survivor of the galleon *Concepción.* This led him to the Ambrosia Banks. Out of provisions, Phips was forced to abandon his search and return to England. King Charles II had died while Phips was at sea and the new King, James II, had Phips imprisoned for his failure.

Once out of prison, Phips was able to persuade the Duke of Albermarle to back his search for the lost treasure of the *Concepcion*. The Duke backed the project, and William Phips set sail from England once more with two ships, the 10-ton, fifty-gun frigate, *Henry of London* and the 200-ton, twenty-two gun *James and Mary*.

Phips provisioned in the New World at Puerto Plata, then sent Commander Francis Rogers in the *Henry*, north to search. Hunting in the shallow banks at 20° 37' North latitude, one of Commander Rogers' divers accidentally found a silver bar when he dove down to take a colorful sea fan. The wreckage of the *Concepcion* itself had been covered with coral growth. Divers aboard the *Henry* found silver bars and coins in the wreck site at depths that ranged from 35 to 50 feet.

Phips joined Commander Rogers on the location and worked the site, using divers and grapnels from the surface. Work on the treasure site lasted two months. Phips was joined by other ships from English colonies in Jamaica and Bermuda. Fearing mutiny from his crew and attack by pirates, Phips gave up the salvage operation and set sail for England. His fortune was made. Phips was acclaimed a hero, knighted and made High Sheriff of Massachusetts. The Royal talley logged 27,556 pounds of silver, 25 pounds of gold, and 37,538 pounds of pieces of eight, silver plate, jewels, and other items.

Phips mounted another salvage fleet, but when he returned to the site, it was being worked by dozens of vessels. The pickings grew slim and Phips was thwarted by primitive salvage means and the coral growth over the wreckage. Phips left the Silver Banks this second time with very little treasure and never again returned.

Convinced that Phips had only scratched the surface in his early salvage of the *Concepcion,* treasure hunters have for years tried to find the legendary wreck. They met with little success until an American born in Annville, Pennsylvania, collaborated with British author Peter Earle, who had located the original log book of Phips' second ship, the *Henry of London* in the Kent Archive in Maidston, England.

With Earle's information from the log of the *Henry*, Burt Webber, using a Varian cesium magnetometer, located the coral-encrusted wreckage on what is now Half Moon Reef. Webber and his divers have found hundreds of silver coins, gold jewelry, silver bars, heavy gold chain necklaces, and a rare astrolabe valued alone at over $100,000.

ANCIENT SHIPWRECKS

Ancient shipwrecks dating from early Roman civilizations have lured Mediterranean divers in quest of amphora, pottery, and priceless historic statuary over centuries.

We had discovered the wreckage of a small Roman merchant ship that had apparently smashed upon the rocks on a remote section of a Spanish reef near Cabo Creus. It is in this section of the coastline that the peninsula veers sharply, creating a narrow passage between the mainland and a stark rocky outcropping known to early sailors as the Maza de Oro.

The existence of the wreck site came to my attention as I observed the conspicuous and mysterious disappearance of a friend and fellow underwater instructor after we completed teaching students to dive each afternoon. He was so secretive that on one afternoon I climbed on the cliffs overlooking the coastline and watched my stealthy companion take our rubber Zodiac dive boat out of the harbor, around the rocks and anchor in a little bay nearby.

With the mystery solved, I quickly offered to document the events of this clandestine salvage on film. Since my friend had come to the point in his operation where he could do no more by hand, he was willing to accept my proposal if I would help him disconnect the village's sewage treatment plant pump and carry it down the cliffs to the harbor. We would use the pump to power a water jet, enabling us to clear away the heavy layer of debris over the wreck. My friend had to admit the manager of the sewage treatment plant, also a diver, in order to have access to the equipment, then only for several hours Sunday, since even the lure of a sunken Roman galleon wouldn't offset the consequences of an overflowing sewage-holding tank.

We set about our salvage operation in earnest, secretly making plans for Sunday. Another diver was recruited when we discovered the sewer pump was too heavy for three to carry down the steep cliffs. It was agreed well in advance that my colleagues would not start foraging with the water jet below until I had an opportunity to photograph the wreck. This was my first real awakening into the world of treasure and divers.

By the time I had adjusted my underwater camera and rolled backwards off our dive boat, the three foragers were in the water and the snaking coils of hose were belching bellows of sand and silt up toward the surface. I couldn't find the bottom let alone my treasure-hunting friends. I managed to shoot a roll of sooty pictures, mostly of arms and legs protruding from clouds of sand.

The second dive of the day was entirely more civilized, but only because my friends didn't find any gold or silver on the first dive. Fish swarmed over the reef, picking at small animals driven out of their homes by the assault of the water jet. Underwater excavation of a shipwreck, even those undertaken with some care, disrupts and destroys large tracts of reef area.

I posed proudly with my treasure-hunting friends as we snapped pictures of each other on the dock, boasting an assortment of pottery, amphora, and masses of fused material which, when later broken apart revealed early ship's tools, a lead anchor, and other artifacts.

Discovery of any underwater wreck site of potentially historic significance should be coupled with responsibility to permit excavation and recovery with a view toward properly documenting the find and preserving the artifacts. The environment of the reef or underwater site must also be considered and potential damage minimized. No doubt there will always be young divers with zeal and a sewer pump, but in most cases that enthusiasm for discovery can be harnessed by a responsible museum, archaeologist or historical society who can make good use of amateurs with underwater skills.

HARBOR ARCHAEOLOGY

Not as exotic as Roman shipwrecks, treasure galleons or lost cities is the cultural heritage forgotten in our bays and harbors abutting the oceans. Commerce evolved from seafaring, and seafaring consumed ships. When man was done with these boats, they were forgotten, beached or burned, salvaged for their metal parts and planking or just put aside someplace and left.

I participated in a project to document and identify, and, if warranted, to remove shipwrecks of historical significance around New York Harbor. The project was part of an environmental assessment being made by the U.S. Army Corps of Engineers. The Corps of Engineers wanted to remove the wreckage chocking the bays and mud flats surrounding New York Harbor. This wreckage was breaking free at high tide and endangering navigation in the Harbor with flotsam. The state of New Jersey also wanted to convert the marshland on the waterfront in one area into a park.

Participating in this cultural assessment of the old ships were the National Maritime Historical Society and the South Street Seaport Museum. Recruited for the project was Peter Throckmorton, famed underwater archaeologist, fresh from his exploits of discovery of early

Greek shipwrecks in the Mediterranean with George Bass.

One of the most fascinating aspects of the survey was the wide variety of life that existed in the intertidal areas and marshland. Rich growth of *Spartina alterniflora* and *Spartina patens* grasses flourished. The wetlands supported a variety of life including marine birds and shellfish one would not have thought able to exist in the polluted harbor.

Local people found crabs prolific and regularly trapped them for food. The Black Tom area we were studying on the Jersey side of the Harbor was named for an oysterman who worked the shallow banks in the early days. Before pollution took its toll, these banks were a productive shellfishing and fishing area. Even now, physical aspects of these marshes around the harbor were quite beautiful and productive. Long-term industrial pollution with chemicals and heavy metals made it dangerous to consume any shellfish or sea life taken in the harbor area, although many persons did so out of need.

With Pete Throckmorton, Dr. Simeon Hook and Dr. Ira Abrams, recently with the University of Pennsylvania Department of Archaeology, we examined the derelicts and wooden shipwrecks with an enthusiasm of discovery. We found mysteries that even the best archaeological detective work couldn't seem to unravel.

An old wooden steamer, thought at first to be the *Newton*, and thus the last remaining Ferris-type wooden steamer in existence, defied positive identification. There was no documentation on her beams and anyone that would have remembered when the ship was abandoned in the marshland was long since dead. The wooden hull was in a good state of preservation, the harbor pollution making it impossible for the wood-boring teredo worm to exist. When Dr. Hook of the Corps of Engineers unearthed an old aerial photograph of New York Harbor taken at a time when the *Newton* was still in commission with the U.S. Navy, the identity of this old derelict was clouded further, apparently never to be solved. No museum had the resources to remove, let alone restore this old wooden ship, so the contractors were left to break it up, carting the wreckage out to sea in barges to be burned.

Other old ships found abandoned in the marshland appeared to have been converted in the 1850s from other types of vessels. Pete Throckmorton called these watermelon barges, naming them for their shape. Pete supposed they had once been used in the flourishing Erie Canal trade, bringing midwestern grain to the Port of New York to feed the demands of Europe, part of the shipbuilding and seafaring commerce that made America flourish.

Walking among the hulks of long forgotten history, observing the tragedy of years of pollution close at hand, one could only dismay at the waste. We saw so clearly how the water resources served a nation, not only providing food, but the means by which America itself prospered.

The harbor wreck assessment project in New York, what some call contemporary archaeology, is a reminder of an important maritime heritage, a national heritage of a young nation, very nearly lost forever. Finding ships of historic significance abandoned on or near shore in the harbor of New York should suggest useful projects in other localities. Projects to locate, assess, and report on forgotten relics from the age of wind and sail could be undertaken by responsible dive clubs with archaeological interest.

DEEP SEA DIVING

We take diving for granted, assuming that since there are the means at hand to probe far away planets in outer space, there must be submarines able to travel and explore anywhere in the deep ocean. While it is true today that there have been great advances in diving equipment, man's exploration of the oceans has only just begun. It was only after the Second World War that the aqualung became generally available and only recently that the sport of diving, as opposed to the military application, has become accessible.

The advent of reliable equipment accessible to the average person has opened new windows in the sea. Ocean reefs have become available to scientists and students who willingly don scuba gear and descend into the ocean laboratory.

Probably the most famous working divers in the world are the hard hats of the U.S. Navy. Their training in the Anacostia River at Washington, D.C.'s Navy Yard prepares them for the many unpleasant conditions working divers confront every day. Man's intrusion in the sea has required an industry that could support not only exploration, but access to ocean resources. The hard-hat diver has become a symbol of that exploration.

The hard-hat diving helmet has been in use since about 1819, when Augustus Siebe invented a helmet with surface-supplied air pumped below through a hose. Almost a decade later, Siebe closed the system, equipping the diver with a suit and the helmet with valves attached to the surface pump. The equipment has remained virtually unchanged over time. Navy divers still don the Mark V diving helmet and canvas suit weighted with 190 pounds of gear, including an 83-pound weight belt and 17 1/2-pound shoes. Air is supplied by compressors aboard ship. The standard Navy diving rig has been somewhat modified to accomodate Heliox mixtures for deep diving. Heliox, a contraction of words, describes the helium and oxygen mixture required for deep dives. For dives in excess of about 300 feet, the percentage of oxygen breathed under a higher partial pressure must be reduced to avoid poisoning. The helium, an inert gas, is substituted for nitrogen which exists in normal atmosphere but which exerts untoward physiological effects when breathed in the presence of carbon dioxide at depths approaching 5 atmospheres absolute or 120 feet or greater.

Hard-hat divers working in standard gear have an effective working range of about 300 to 350 feet. Decompression for today's hard-hat diver—that is, the programmed stops at gradually diminishing depths on ascent to safely eliminate nitrogen (or helium) gas dissolved in the blood and tissues—occurs aboard ship in decompression chambers. Some chambers are equipped with modern conveniences in order to minimize the psychological strain required by long decompression after very deep dives.

I watched Navy divers and tenders train against a stop watch, simulating bringing a full dressed hard-hat diver to the surface, removing the heavy and cumbersome helmet and gear and getting the diver into the ship's decompression chamber before the minutes elapsed. Three minutes is all the time Navy Dive Tables allow on the surface before mandatory decompression must begin in order to avoid the dreaded bends. In this drill, the Navy men worked quickly and efficiently, wasting no movements, keenly aware that once their training was over, the lives of the divers would depend on the efficiency and speed of their work.

The alternative to a dry decompression chamber aboard ship, with television, a chess board, cot and medical technicians in attendance in the event of an emergency, would be the dismal prospect of making stops at different depths in the water as the diver surfaces. The diver would have to wait at these stops until the Navy tables indicate the diver can ascend to the next stop or surface.

Sport scuba divers who have gone deep enough or stayed long enough to require decompression can well attest to the discomfort, especially in cold water, of waiting out long minutes of decompression underwater. For deep dives to extreme depths, common fare for the working professional diver, this decompression may require many hours.

North Sea oil platforms, underwater pipelines, pier construction, salvage and sundry underwater jobs occupy the modern working diver. While sponge boats still put out each season from the Greek port of Kalymnos, their frail wooden hulls and frayed equipment hardly compare with the new gear oil companies and their diving contractors stow in the lockers aboard offshore oil rigs. But the men are very much the same: workers in the sea, earning a livelihood from the oceans in a profession frought with danger, daring to intrude into the ocean's depths in order that mankind can harvest the sea's resources.

SUBMARINES AND SUBMERSIBLES

Submarine makers have tried for centuries to perfect a device that would enable men to conquer the rigors and hazards of deep water exploration. Much of the impetus for building submarines over history came as part of man's warring. The fallout of submarine technology has been the development of submersibles for peace time use.

Homer wrote about military diving activities in the *Iliad* in 700 B.C., and statutes in Rhodes as early as the third century B.C. regulated the payment of treasure shares to divers depending on the depth and risk.

Exploits in submarine warfare began with the use of diving bells. Soldiers of Alexander the Great in 333 B.C. used a diving bell to destroy a boom installed for the defense of Tyre. In the fourth century B.C., Aristotle wrote about a diving kettle or bell.

By the end of the seventeenth century, elaborate diving bells were being used to recover treasure. William Phips used one to give his divers more bottom time as they salvaged the treasure of the *Concepcion*.

Patents were issued to Edmund Halley in 1691 for a diving bell which could be replenished by casks of fresh air lowered in barrels lined with lead. With the advent of the use of pumps, these diving bells became a practical reality, enabling divers to remain below the surface to perform productive work.

Deep ocean exploits of William Beebe, descending to a depth of 3,084 feet, lowered in a bathysphere in 1934, heralded a new horizon for ocean exploration. On January 23, 1960, diving in the bathyscape *Trieste*, Jacques Piccard and Lieutenant Don Walsh reached a depth of 35,800 feet diving in the Mariana Trench in the Pacific, the deepest ever attained in the ocean.

Subsequent explorations by Jacques Piccard and others helped develop a new genre of undersea submersible that could remain underwater for months at a time, gathering biological and environmental data. In July 1969, Piccard and a crew of five scientists and pilots, descended in the submersible *Ben Franklin* in the warm Gulf Stream waters off West Palm Beach, Florida. The scientists remained submerged thirty days and eleven hours, drifting underwater northward with the Gulf Stream current, observing marine life through twenty-nine portholes in the submersible.

The *Ben Franklin* finally surfaced 360 miles south of Nova Scotia, having covered 1444 nautical miles at an average depth of 650 feet. During the trip, scientists collected over 900,000 temperature, salinity, and sound velocity measurements and 500 temperature versus depth profiles of the Gulf Stream, adding immeasurably to information on physical and biological aspects of the Atlantic.

In addition to the valuable data obtained from the Gulf Stream drift mission, the spirit of submarine use for scientific pursuits received a great boost and favorable worldwide publicity. The *Ben Franklin* mission spawned a number of independent ventures in submarine building around the world.

Tiny diving saucers able to descend to 1200 feet were popularly used by divers like Jacques Cousteau to film natural phenomena of the ocean never before seen. Life was discovered at depths where, previously, science could only speculate on the basis of scanty evidence recovered by deep sea grabs and trawls. Slowly, divers began to search out deeper ocean areas, recording their exploits on film. This data has changed and reshaped scientific theory about environmental habits and ecological relationships in the deep ocean.

These tiny submarines maintained a cabin pressure of one atmosphere, the same pressure as at the surface, so operators were not required to undergo decompression.

Two of the best-known submersible and undersea research vehicle builders in the world are located in Florida. One, the Harbor Branch Foundation, is a private nonprofit ocean research organization located on the Indian River at Fort Pierce. The other, Perry Oceanographic, of West Palm Beach, is a private venture engaging in contract research and the development of undersea vehicles for industry.

Harbor Branch became operational in 1970 with science and ocean-engineering laboratories, shipyards, and research facilities. Priority projects at Harbor Branch concern the use of submersibles to transport scientists to the ocean bottom where they can do productive work, finally being returned safely to the surface.

The Johnson-Sea-Link submersible aboard the mother ship Sea Diver. The submarine is operated by the Harbor Branch Foundation for scientific ocean research. This submarine was used by researchers to reconnoiter and take pictures of the Civil War ironclad ship Monitor, sunk off Cape Hatteras.

Harbor Branch was founded with the patronage of J.S. Johnson. Ed Link, underwater submersible pioneer and ocean explorer, joined Harbor Branch and together with other researchers began developing a new class of underwater submarine, the Johnson Sea Link.

A tragic accident in 1973 which claimed the life of Ed Link's son, off Key West, Florida, when his submarine became entangled in cable at 360-feet and was disabled, impelled Harbor Branch's activities in devising submarine rescue vehicles. This activity resulted in the invention of an unmanned submarine rescue device called the Cabled Observation and Rescue Device (CORD). The rescue submarine is operated remotely by a sophisticated electronic guidance system. CORD is capable of locking rescue cables onto a disabled submersible so that it can be brought up to the surface.

Divers using Harbor Branch submersibles have recently recovered artifacts from the Civil War ironclad *Monitor*, sunk off Cape Hatteras, North Carolina in 1863. Divers were locked out over the *Monitor*, working tethered to the submarine at depths of 210 feet.

109

When the divers completed photographing the shipwreck and later excavating a portion of the wreck site, they returned to the submarine and were kept at ambient pressure, that is actual saturation pressure of the working depth. The isolated pilot's compartment in the sub, protected by a thick plexiglass viewing port, was maintained at surface pressure. Thus when the submersible's pilot brought his vessel to the surface the pilot required no decompression at all. Once the submersible was hoisted aboard and the hatch coupled, the men in the separate diving compartment were transferred through the hatch, still under pressure, to a large chamber aboard the Research Vessel Johnson. This permitted the *Monitor* divers to eliminate accumulated inert gas safely and in relative comfort.

In similar projects, scientists have been locked out of Johnson Sea Link submersibles to take water samples, examine marine life and study environmental effects associated with pollution. This new breed of submarine, designed for use of marine biologists and oceanographers has put the deep ocean within range of close study. Organisms can be observed in their natural habitat and important studies made in areas beyond the effective range of divers using scuba gear or cumbersome diving suits. Exploration of areas where the physical ocean elements make exposure of the human diver impossible is being accomplished by sophisticated submarines, adding to our knowledge of the sea.

8

Environmental Problems

"We have acquired not only the ability to exploit the oceans' resources much better but also, by overfishing and polluting, to destroy the ocean's capacity to sustain life, to waste the mineral potential of the seas, and to degrade the marine environment far from where an ocean activity takes place," commented John R. Stevenson, America's former Chief Delegate to the United Nations Law of the Sea Conference, describing the need for a new level of awareness about the environmental problems faced by the marine environment.

Pollution is all pervasive, reaching the oceans in several general ways: by direct dumping; indirectly by contaminated rivers or estuaries; as runoff or leachate from the land; and by precipitation from the atmosphere, vaporized pollutants congealing in raindrops and falling back to Earth.

While mankind is looking to the sea to support ever growing population demands for food, the productiveness of these great ocean resources have been and are being seriously affected by pollution. Overharvesting and physical destruction have also taken a toll on ocean resources. As science continues to define subtle nuances caused by pollution, we realize too late that we have upset a fragile balance in the sea that is directly tied to our own survival.

TOXIC WASTES, A PERMANENT PERIL

The driver backed a 7,000 gallon tank truck up against a wooden railroad tie. The tie was supported by a rusting bolt, part of a deteriorated pier, the degenerating cement crumbling and the rotting tie vibrating under the weight of the tank truck. The driver got out of his truck, walked back to the end of the decayed pier, put one foot on the rotting railroad tie and cautiously looked around. Satisfied that the coast was clear, the driver unhooked the tank truck's hoses, attached the couplings, opened the truck's ventilating hatch, and with one more furtive look around, threw the end of the hose down into the water of Kill Van Kull. In the next instant, the driver started the truck's high pressure pump.

Police detectives, watching through long-lens surveillance cameras across on the other side of the waterway, saw vapor come out of the tank truck's venting hatch. This signaled that the truck was being emptied. The police detectives called their stake-out teams on a walkie-talkie and told them to move in.

This case had a more or less happy ending. The truck driver was arrested for illegally dumping his load of poisonous chemical wastes into a tributary that led directly into the Atlantic Ocean, through the Bay. The arrest only meant that investigators caught one dumper in one act of illegally and dangerously disposing of toxic industrial chemical waste. It also meant that the criminal conduct had been going on unchecked for years.

The consequences of untold numbers of cases involving clandestine dumping of toxic waste into the oceans cannot be gauged. The results of these poisonings may not even be known for a generation or more. The effects of many of these industrial wastes on human health and the marine environment is only beginning to be understood in a most tragic way: a permanent, irreversible contamination of the food chain by substances that cause deformities, mutations, disease and ecological disruption on a large scale.

Using the most recent government estimates, these highly toxic byproducts of industry are generated at a rate of some 56 million metric tons per year. In two of the major areas of high population density and industrialization, both abutting the Atlantic Ocean, 4.6 million metric tons of hazardous wastes are generated in the State of New Jersey, and 3.5 million metric tons are generated in New York per year.

Huge quantities of these dangerous wastes have been dumped into the oceans. In the state of New Jersey alone, of a total of 1.2 billion gallons of hazardous waste generated in only one year, six hundred million gallons of this highly toxic waste were poured into the Atlantic Ocean.

These staggering figures represent only the "legitimate" dumping of hazardous waste. This means the ocean dumping that has been permitted by environmental officials and reported. The countless millions or billions of gallons of hazardous waste that is disposed of each year by clandestine means, in ways such as those described above, goes untallied.

Flying into New York's Kennedy Airport recently on a clear day, I was appalled to look down and see miles of ocean, far out off the New Jersey coast, stained with yellow streaks. These streaks were clear visual evidence of the chemical dumping that has been going on virtually unchecked for years. Now, when the untoward results of such reckless conduct can no longer be disputed, the dumping continues because industry complains there are no other means available to safely dispose of this toxic waste or the means are too costly to employ.

A recent investigative report summarized the way these toxic wastes are handled in the United States in the following terms: "Environmentally unsound, dangerous, illegal and deliberately improper practices in generating, transporting, treating, storing and disposing of hazardous wastes and solid wastes by certain elements have contaminated the land and water, caused disease, including birth defects, mutations in children, cancer, miscarriages, liver damage, and other diseases, leading to death and degeneration of human and animal health and have created irreversible damage to elements of the environment. These improper and dangerous practices are flagrant and widespread."

Within the framework of this situation, the U.S. Environmental Protection Agency has found that "over 90% of the hazardous waste generated in the United States today is handled improperly and may be or is causing detrimental effects to human health and the environment every day."

These reports paint a grim picture of the present status of the way toxic wastes are handled. The prospects are even more grim when one considers that these abuses are occurring at a time when the most progressive of the industrial nations of the world is at the height of modern technology. In the past, all of these toxic wastes were dumped into the ocean and mankind blissfully disregarded the consequences. With some notion of the consequences, it seems that environmental concern has not been able to keep pace with the inherent desire for industry to turn a profit, in spite of future consequences.

Clouds of pink and mauve leachate oozed into the marshland. Oily, blackened material bubbled out of the swamp. When the chemicals mixed, they reflected the sunlight in a kaleidoscope of colors against the green reeds and dull fall sky. The tide rose and fell, and the waters of the creek lapped against the newly dumped chemical mess, peeling away superficial layers of dirt dumped on the ground to conceal the massive illegal dumping in a protected marshland.

From a helicopter, there could be no mistake. The trail from the dump site into the creek, thence into the riverway that led to the ocean was clear. Yet because of the clever way in which the dumping was done, the creek waters, acted on by strong tides, diluted the chemical waste so that the Coast Guard investigators would not readily see the massive discoloration coming out all at once. Progressive lines of color streaked their way into the ocean, continually diluted until they were invisible to the naked eye.

These illegal chemical dump sites, on marsh lands, off backwaters and bays, provided an almost perfect cover for illegal dumping activities. Front companies had been set up. They held themselves out as treaters of chemical waste, and thus collected thousands of dollars from major industrial concerns to haul away and dispose of, in an environmentally sound manner, these toxic wastes. Since chemical processes to neutralize poisonous waste can be quite costly, the persons that ran unlawful dump sites solved the problem by simply dumping out back into the marshland, caring not at all that it migrated into the ocean. The net profit per truck load of chemicals amounted to around $15,000. The net damage to marine life as a result of this unlawful dumping is incalculable.

Electric capacitors and transformers make use of polychlorinated biphenyls (PCBs). PCBs are extremely dangerous to human and animal health, having been found to cause cancer. Like many dangerous chemical substances, once manufactured, they can only be destroyed or broken down by elaborate chemical or physical means. PCBs are biocumulative, which means once disposed or once they enter the food chain, they remain in their original state, accumulating without breaking down. This cumulative effect of continued exposure to PCBs increases the risk of disease.

Over a period of years, a large company involved in the manufacture of electrical equipment for industry discharged its PCB waste directly into the Hudson River about 40 miles north of Albany. The New York State Department of Environmental Conservation granted

114

the company a permit. The PCB discharge flowed toward the Atlantic with the river, some of the wastes settling into the sediment on the bottom. The Hudson supported a significant commercial and sport fishing industry but, because of the PCB contamination, the government had to ban most commercial fishing in the river. When the extent of the contamination became known, the company retreated behind its state permit, and the state averred that the company should have stopped discharging the waste once they found out PCBs were toxic.

In the end, the massive contamination of the Hudson, one of the most important tributaries on the East coast flowing into the Atlantic and supporting a wide variety of life, has directly effected the quality of human life. It has deprived man of important food resources and has poisoned the food chain with contaminants that can only be removed by expensive dredging of sediment. The problem remains unresolved as environmental specialists ponder the fate of the river, debating how government will raise at least 30 million dollars to undertake the dredging and removal of the PCB laden sediment. As for the major industrial company that caused the pollution, they quickly settled with New York by payment of some 4 million dollars as reparation. The Hudson PCB contamination underlines the crisis caused by poisoned rivers running to the sea. Corps of Engineers specialists informed me that the sediment dredged from New York Harbor contains high levels of PCBs, an invariable result of the contamination far upstream.

Without fully realizing the ecological consequences, dangerous chemicals and industrial wastes have been haphazardly deposited on the land or buried in landfill sites. Ironically, since we disdain the unaesthetic character of garbage dumps, often fearing their inherent adverse health consequences, landfill sites are most often located in areas of little human habitation or on land considered to have little commerical value. This has almost always meant, for the populous states abutting the oceans or waterways, that the landfill or dump would be located in a swampy area, on a marshland, along a "useless" stretch of harbor, on a mud flat or bay leading to the ocean that was considered of little value.

Part of the thinking that went into decisions of where to locate garbage dumps included schemes to use the waste to landfill these areas, eventually turning the "worthless" swamp, marsh or mud flat into a commercial piece of real estate.

Years after the implementation of this philosophy regarding the siting of landfills, water resource experts are expressing dismay at the environmental damage this careless siting has caused. These massive dump sites have been and are causing untold environmental damage to the marine environment, often upsetting the delicate balance that exists in the oceans.

While no one completely understands what it is that triggers an imbalance or what saturation limits of foreign materials will destroy that balance, it is clear to any scientific observer that these landburial sites pose a grave environmental hazard.

Leachate is a term used by sanitary engineers to describe the concentrated, highly polluted liquid that exudes from a landfill. Leachate is the result of degeneration of the material dumped coming in contact with water or other liquid flowing through the garbage. Leachate in most cases concentrates poisonous matter, including toxic heavy metals. Leachate poses a perpetual environmental hazard for many years after the landfill has been closed or abandoned. Where chemical or industrial waste has been dumped into the landfill, the leachate problem is compounded and its toxicity increased. Even those landfill sites used as receptacles for household refuse cause dangerous contamination as a result of the leachate concentrating lead, mercury, arsenic and other highly poisonous substances.

The majority of landfill sites, even in places far from the seas, have been located in areas thought to have little commercial value, without regard to the type of soil or water table over which they were situated. Rarely was there any concern for the landfill's proximity to ground water aquifers or water resources.

Environmental engineers studying what have been denominated "state of the art secure landburial sites" for highly toxic waste have recently reported that the histories "of these types of facilities have been all bad." These experts have concluded that secure landfills are "abysmal" means for isolating wastes from the environment.

Reporting on some recent observations of toxic waste landfill sites, a government environmental engineer indicated that he witnessed levels of leachate within the landfills' chambers which had risen to the brim. The engineer reported strong odors of volatile organic chemicals being emitted and 300,000 gallons of poisonous leachate which had to be pumped out of a series of closed "secure" landfills in order to prevent the toxic matter from contaminating the environment.

Exudate, contaminated with deadly poisons, is often seen pouring out of landfill sites, the flow sometimes resembling mini-rivers. These rivers of leachate often flow directly into the oceans, or indirectly into the oceans via swamplands, marshes or tributaries. Landfill sites that have received industrial toxic wastes are far more dangerous than garbage dumps, but because of the toxic nature of leachate, pollution of water resources has occurred and is increasing on a dangerous scale from all categories of landfills.

The dramatic pictures showing a Japanese mother holding her deformed child, remain poignant in the memory of many persons who read the photo-journalistic chronicle of mercury poisoning in Minamata, Japan. The Minamata tragedy was caused by a factory dumping mercury wastes into bay and ocean waters and the subsequent harvesting and consumption of mercury-contaminated fish and shellfish from those waters by the populace. This disaster is often cited as a classic example of how toxic wastes enter the food chain and not only affect the environment, but present human health hazards including loss of vision, cerebral damage, weakening of the musculature, coma and paralysis.

These tragic examples brutally disarm those that characterize persons who express environmental concerns as eccentrics. Attitudes change slowly, even in the face of human tragedy. The photographer who documented the Minamata disaster was physically beaten up because of his efforts to expose the problem.

Only recently, in a small New Jersey community, the spectre of a tragedy like that at Minamata has caused concern and consternation over what to do with a long abandoned mercury dump site on land abutting Berry's Creek, a tributary of the Hackensack River which flows into Newark Bay and thence into the Atlantic.

The problem involving the Wood Ridge, New Jersey mercury site arose sometime prior to World War II and continued for almost 40 years. A succession of chemical companies from 1937 to 1973 engaged in the business of manufacturing mercury on the site adjacent to the creek. Over the years, quantities of mercury spilled onto the ground, or were dumped out, or various mercury containing wastes were disposed of outside the old factory or into the creek. In 1973, the old mercury factory buildings were abandoned, leveled to make room for a large food packaging plant. While everyone concerned knew of the existence of the old mercury plant on the site and the contamination, nothing was done about the problem. Years later, in 1979, tests were made of the area, responding to renewed environmental concerns that the mercury was in the creek bed and theoretically could contaminate the Atlantic fisheries off the New Jersey coast. Officials reported finding the highest concentrations of mercury anyplace in the world in the ground adjacent to Berry's Creek and in the creek bed. Responsible officials estimated that from 200 to 400 tons of mercury are present in this small area.

The mercury contamination threat has not yet been solved to the satisfaction of responsible officials in this small New Jersey community. The situation presents another example how indirect acts hold the potential for dangerous contamination of our waters, and how once despoiled by toxic substances like mercury, the oceans' food resources cannot be consumed.

In simpler terms yet, one need only ask the gourmet why swordfish was removed from the menus of seafood restaurants. It was a result of contamination of the swordfish with mercury.

The world has come to equate the words Love Canal with human tragedy resulting from years of dumping of dangerous chemical wastes into an abandoned power canal. The dump site was subsequently covered with dirt and the land used for a housing development and elementary school. What is less apparent and only beginning to pay tragic dividends miles from the dumping site is the migration of these toxic chemicals out of Love Canal into the Niagara River, presenting potential contamination of major water resources.

SEWAGE WASTES

Charles Stratton, a veteran charter boat captain and diver has, for some twenty years, made observations of the Atlantic Ocean off the New York and New Jersey coastlines where he regularly plies his deep diving trade. Stratton has repeatedly complained that raw sewage was being dumped into the ocean by municipalities, evading pollution guidelines.

In 1976, diving with Charlie Stratton and the president of the American Littoral Society, twenty miles out in the Atlantic, we observed a massive fish kill on the bottom. We swam over large areas of the bottom, through thick flocculent matter suspended in the water. We were over a shallow area of the Continental Shelf. Documenting the disaster, we found that everything was dead. Lobster, some weighing up to twenty pounds, denizens that had survived eighty or a hundred years of life in the ocean, were dead on the bottom. Starfish and mussels were dead, fish were dead or dying, sedentary marine animals were also dead or dying. We took samples of the dead marine life for laboratory testing.

In his inimitable fashion, Charlie Stratton disdained the laboratory tests, averring that he had been predicting the present state of affairs for years. It appeared, however, that the massive fish kill was as bad or worse than Charlie's prognosis. Commercial fishermen reported

Charles Stratton and Dave Bulloch examine evidence of a massive fish kill in the Atlantic. Dave was then President of the American Litoral Society.

running many miles over the fishing banks with no results. Draggers and scallop fishermen were coming back with harrowing tales of dead sea life.

Our discovery was reported in the press, and I wrote articles describing the conditions we had observed. When the situation was sorted out some months later, the conditions that created this massive ocean-life kill was called an inversion.

The causes of an inversion can be complex, but it appears, as best as science can sort it out, that algae growing in great numbers, feeding off sewage, created this massive oceanographic disturbance. These algae suffocated other marine life as they died and bacteria attacked them, using up the available oxygen in the process, causing the massive ocean-life kill. As a result of this one particular ocean problem, commercial fisheries lost $264 million, and a $90 million annual shellfishing industry was closed. Bluefish did not migrate into the waters north of Brielle, New Jersey; there were no sea bass, porgies and only a few summer flounder in the traditional fishing grounds. Many flounder came into the shallows and were seen

119

breaking the surface for air. Fishermen on shore took many of these hapless flatfish, so unusual was the condition, and so easy the pickings. Trawlers ran out as far as 90 or 100 miles into the ocean seeking clean water. Finally and tragically, the plight of the oceans was being brought home. Bad news at a time when mankind was beginning to express fear that the world's food resources would not be sufficient to feed an ever growing world population.

Sewage sludge, the concentrated residue from waste treatment plants, has been routinely dumped in the Atlantic Ocean off Ambrose Light for more than 40 years. This sludge from the New York City metropolitan area is towed by barge into an area of the ocean known as the New York Bight and discharged. In the vast ocean area of this dumping, nothing lives. It is called the "dead sea." Ships' captains have been rumored to anchor over the site in order that barnacles, algae and other attaching organisms exposed to the contaminated water, devoid of oxygen, would die and drop off the hull.

Over the years, this sludge has been migrating over the bottom and recent observation has found dumped matter as close as ¼ mile off New York's barrier beaches on Long Island. While there has been a great deal of concern about this ocean dumping, officials have calculated that this sewage sludge, generated in the amount of 4.5 to 5 million cubic yards per year, if deposited on the land, would cover an area the size of Brooklyn and Queens (about 185 square miles) with a layer of goo 2 inches deep. These same officials complain that if the sludge were dumped on the land, the land would become contaminated, and disease-carrying organisms not killed by routine chlorination would affect human health.

What prognosis this leaves for the ocean repositories of this unpleasant matter is not altogether clear. What is clear is that much of the ocean, even with its amazing dilution and dispersing abilities, has been saturated, in some areas, beyond environmentally safe limits by this dumping. The result has been a large dead sea, incapable of supporting life, incapable of coming back even if dumping stopped.

"Look at the price of fish, that's all," my friend Charlie Stratton declares, when he gets to talking about the adverse impact dumping has had on the ocean's ability to support life. "You don't need fancy scientific reasons. Just look at the catch. They've been covering it up for a long time now, don't want to turn people away at the markets. What they do catch, I won't eat it," Stratton declared one day, holding his nose while bending over unhealthy shellfish we brought up from the Atlantic bottom for submission to a testing laboratory.

In the end, I suppose Charlie Stratton has simplified the issue as well as anyone can. Pollution has spoiled the ocean, and this spoilage has resulted in a decrease in the ocean's ability to support life. As ocean food resources decrease, the price of food goes up. It was surely true from our discussions with commercial fishermen who regularly work the waters of the Continental Shelf off America's East Coast. They were running longer distances from port, staying away longer and catching fewer fish.

Was this massive fish kill in the Atlantic off the New York and New Jersey coasts the direct result of the sewage dumping? While some governmental officials remained noncommittal, attributing the massive ocean-life kill to "complex ocean environment factors," men like Charlie Stratton, whose lives bring them to the ocean week after week, have no doubts about the cause. Charlie tells about how when he first dove the Atlantic waters perhaps twenty years ago, he could look down from the surface and see the shipwrecks shimmering on the sand, eighty or a hundred feet below.

The last time we dove together, out some 20 miles in the Atlantic, the water was murky, brown flocculent matter clouded visibility. Material was in suspension, and worse, when we examined the bottom, miles from the site of sewage-sludge dumping, the sand contained a black matter that had settled down into the bottom resembling sulfide. When we scooped up the sandy bottom, the black material was stirred up and became suspended in the water.

In addition to barge-hauled sludge, municipal waste treatment plants pump their waste water and sewage directly into the ocean. Each day, 400 to 600 million gallons of raw and partly treated sewage has been and presently is discharged into New York Harbor. Studying the effects of this dumping on the area coastal zone's $340-million-a-year fishing industry, officials of the New England Fisheries Center have found dangerous levels of heavy metals in the water and ocean sediment.

Heavy metals in significantly elevated concentrations were considered to present an imminent threat to the more than 15,000-square-mile area of the New York Bight, extending from Montauk, Long Island to Cape May, New Jersey. Lead, cadmium, mercury, organics containing PCBs, insecticides such as DDT and copper were found in the sediment of New York and Raritan Bays, in Long Island Sound, and out into the Atlantic. Scientists found these contaminants had entered the food chain, and, in some cases, had been the cause of death of bottom-dwelling marine organisms.

The effects of heavy metals are cumulative. Scientists found concentrations of 100 to 800 parts per million of heavy metals which should not exceed 1 to 3 parts per million. Taken together, the heavy metals in the areas tested represented dangerous concentrations.

Raritan Bay was devoid of bottom-dwelling shrimp which abounded there in the early 1960s. These shrimp supported bass and flatfish. The shrimp are gone as are the food fish.

Major commercial fish stocks were found contaminated with PCBs. In some areas, food fish stocks were nonexistent.

DREDGE SPOIL

In addition to this massive dumping of sewage sludge and raw or partially treated sewage, the ocean bottom is being silted over as the result of dredging and the dumping of dredged material.

"The wrecks are disappearing into it," Charlie Stratton declared. "She sits barely 3 feet out of the silt. Was a time the wreck was 10 feet out of the bottom. That's silting in. It's covering the bottom, suffocating life," Stratton continued, describing vividly the results of construction and dredge spoil dumping in the Atlantic.

There is a dredge spoil dump site in the Atlantic about 6 miles off the New Jersey coast. The dump site is under the jurisdiction of the U.S. Army Corps of Engineers which has permitted from about 7 to 11 million cubic yards of dumping each year. The Corps of Engineers reported that 7 million cubic yards were from dredging New York Harbor where sediment from the Hudson River, contaminated with PCBs and other pollutants accumulate.

The dredge spoil dump area along the Atlantic's Hudson Shelf Valley combines with the sewage dumping and ocean dumping of acid wastes to contaminate one of the most important ocean areas in the world.

Responding to Federal environmental requirements, the Corps of Engineers has developed contract laboratories which have artificially created conditions where the effects of dredge spoil can be tested. The laboratories expose marine organisms to varying levels of heavy metals found in the sediments and report their findings to the Corps.

The Marine Protection, Research and Sanctuaries Act of 1972 (PL 92-532) imposes the burden on the dumpers to make ecological evaluations of dredged material they propose to dump in the ocean. The laboratory techniques and standards are being developed every day. It is a new field and even with the most sophisticated means science can not judge the effects toxic wastes and hazardous materials will have on the ocean environment and its inhabitants five, ten, or even fifty years from now. That a toxin does not kill a fish, shrimp, or mussel does not mean that the problem is solved. That a chemical substance may exert subtle genetic changes generations after its consumption is considered probable, but still not understood. What effects these chemicals will have years hence on the human consumer is also little understood.

The problem of disposing of dredge spoil and other material is not easily simplified nor easily disregarded. Harbors and bays must be kept navigable and that is the Corps of Engineers job. The material dredged must be disposed someplace, that too is the Corps job. In none of this is there an oceanographic crystal ball to say how things will turn out. No crystal ball is needed, however, to note the present and pervasive bad effects of present dumping on the oceans and to predict bad news in the future.

GOVERNMENT AS A MAJOR POLLUTER

Goals and deadlines to prohibit ocean dumping entirely have been set. Most of these deadlines have been overrun and ignored as soon as they appeared to loom on the calendar. Those sectors that should be the most environmentally conscious and ecologically responsible are often the most flagrant offenders of ocean-dumping rules. Often laws are not enforced against municipalities or cities which continue to dump sewage into the ocean in violation of Federal dumping standards.

Charlie Stratton, increasingly dismayed at bureaucratic tolerance of government violation of ocean-dumping standards, decided one year to engage in some spy work for the environmental cause. He signed on as a diver to install a pipeline that would carry sewage waste from a municipal treatment plant out into the ocean. Previously, the outfalls would boil out, concentrating the unpleasant material so as to affect Jersey's amusement park beaches. The municipal administrators wanted to accomplish the same results, without having them visible. Stratton went to work building a long pipe with diffusers or spouts. The pipe was constructed out into the ocean. The diffusers would spread the sewage waste out over a larger area for the entire length of this pipeline. The pipe cost the municipality, according to Stratton, a million dollars. After the pipeline was built, surge and winter sea caused it to vibrate, bouncing up and down, making it quite evident to Stratton that the million dollars spent to cover up evidence of improperly treated waste being dumped into the ocean was

123

squandered.

"I took buckets of the stuff boiling out of the outfalls. Settleable solids were present in violation of Federal standards. When we confronted them, they had some excuse. Excessive rain made them by-pass treatment or our samples they said were improperly taken. I tell you they are destroying the ocean," Stratton said, describing the common plight of the world's ocean resources.

Since sewage-treatment plants take in storm sewer run-offs from the land, they pass the waste water out through their systems with only primary treatment (chlorination) when the system is overloaded after rain storms. Raw sewage is often directly pumped into the ocean. Pesticides and herbicides are carried, concentrated in these land run-off wastes from storm sewers and are also pumped through the sewer outfalls into the ocean. Very recent experiments have shown, to the pessimistic consternation of researchers, that even minute DDT concentrations in sea water drastically reduce the level of photosynthesis of marine plants. Without the plant producers, an ocean environment would collapse.

POISONED RAIN

The physical law of conservation of energy was a popular generalization in the nineteenth century. James Joule extended this general concept that energy cannot be created nor destroyed to include mechanical, thermal, chemical, electrical, or other energy. Albert Einstein broadened the concept still further in 1905 to equate mass and energy. Using this general concept, since all forms of energy are quantitatively exchangeable with mechanical energy, a substance is not destroyed when it is burned or treated chemically. It doesn't disappear when acted on or reacted with, it simply takes another form.

Material that is incinerated or fumes given off in chemical or manufacturing processes simply convert what were once liquids or solids into volatile form. These vaporized substances enter the atmosphere as smoke or vapor. This diffused matter, suspended and floating in the air, eventually becomes attached to rain droplets. When it rains, these vaporized substances fall back to Earth where they enter the ocean environment.

Acid rain is a term that provokes a great deal of concern among conservationists. On land, the effects of vaporized acid substances, the smokestack effluents of manufacturing, can readily be seen. Great limestone buildings are pock marked and eaten away by these dangerous clouds.

In areas where the poisoned atmosphere is breathed, as in the region of Staten Island, New York, an area that daily receives the wind-borne fumes from New Jersey's chemical and industrial manufacturing, the incidence of human lung and respiratory cancer is among the highest in the world.

More subtly, the vaporized pollutants fall to Earth and accumulate in the ocean environment. The effects of these pollutants are complex. They may be regional, changing the acidity of mountain lakes, effecting local ecological balances, or these air-borne residues may be cumulative, over time upsetting the balance of nature, exceeding the ocean's ability to indefinitely dilute these pollutants and thus spread them harmlessly over a great area.

Incineration has been one of the alternatives to ocean dumping of sewage sludge. While incineration is possible and while there are proposals to use the sludge as fuel alternatives, burning it to turn generating turbines, the emissions, unless carefully controlled could intolerably affect air quality and create pollution of a different form, including heavy metal fall-out. Recent attempts have been made to convert sewage sludge into compost or fertilizer with some success. As long as cheap ocean dumping remains, the feasibility of using other forms of technology to convert sludge will not be pursued.

OIL SPILLS

Petty annoyance maybe, but bathers had to select where they were going to place their beach towels with care. Those who walked or ran along the miles of beautiful coral sand beach would have to stop and look at the soles of their feet, then seek out a shell or piece of drift wood to clean the tar. A couple of bathers, seeing me snorkling over the reefs, asked where all the tar came from on this rather isolated Bahamas beach, miles from thickly populated areas and devoid of industry. The people assumed the tar was somehow connected with boats, most thinking it was a form of loosened caulking from the planks.

Tar balls are unpleasant to most beach goers, found even in remote areas where they spoil some of the picturesque beauty of magnificent white sand beaches. Quite simply, tar balls are formed from congealed oil droplets adhering together, accumulating small bits of other matter and worked round by the ocean. Tar is symptomatic of a larger problem, physical damage caused by oil spillage on the water.

There was a time when ships' captains, having to pay by weight as their vessels would go through the Suez Canal, would pump extra bunker oil out into the sea. As the price of oil increased, this practice became less feasible. Shipping companies would pump the extra bunker into tanks to save both fuel costs and toll costs at the canal.

Rising fuel costs have somewhat spared the oceans from deliberate dumping of oil. Laws regarding oil spill pollution have also contributed to alleviating some of the problem. Still, tanker captains have been cited for ridding their tanks of oil contaminated ballast water by pumping them at sea, thus washing considerable petroleum debris into the ocean. The same is true for captains that pump their bilges. Shipboard oil leaks accumulate petroleum residues, which mix with water any ship takes in its bilges. This contaminated bilge is pumped into the ocean.

The cumulative effect of this purposeful pumping of oil and debris has created a significant pollution problem. Accidents at sea, dockside spills, ruptures at offshore oil-drilling platforms also account for significant ocean pollution. Taking figures amassed by the National Academy of Sciences' Ocean Affairs Board, as much as 10 million metric tons of petroleum products enter the ocean each year. This includes about 600,000 metric tons of oil that seep into the marine environment through faults in the ocean floor.

Oil coats the surface of the water killing marine birds, sea otters, and dozens of larger species that live on the sea. The oil migrates to shore and physically despoils large tracts of beach which support leisure activities and commerce. Some of the environmental problems caused by petroleum product spills have long-term effects on marine life less obvious than physical coating and smothering of organisms.

Many factors influence the impact that a petroleum product spill will have on the marine environment. Spills near shore or in shallow water will have more pervasive effects and do more damage in the intertidal breeding and spawning areas than midocean spills. Spills occurring where there is wave action, which helps the process of evaporation of the spilled material, cause less damage than oil which remains stagnant over an area. Oil spills in the summer or in warm water will have a more severe impact on the marine organisms than a mid-winter spill. In winter, after the spawning season, some organisms, for example, crabs, burrow into the bottom thus avoiding poisoning from material on the surface or in suspension. Of course if settling or sedimentation of the spill occurs, it will cause the winter-burrowing crabs to die.

Aromatic hydrocarbons (benzene or benzene-ring-containing

chemicals) are among the most toxic of petroleum products. In addition to the short-term mortality caused by lower molecular weight aromatics, the higher molecular weight compounds have been found to be carcinogenic in some animal species. Since boiling point increases with higher molecular weights, chemists have been trying to gauge spill damage by analyzing the aromatic content of the petroleum spilled and its boiling point.

Sessile organisms which can seal themselves up like clams or oysters, and not feed for a period of days, may avoid poisoning if a spill is transitory. The offspring or larvae of these organisms, however, will be wiped out. This would hold true for oyster spat. Studies in some salt marshes, where there have been large scale invertebrate kills, have shown the marshland not to have made a recovery as long as three years after the oil spill. The organisms had not reestablished themselves. In some cases, toxic oil was found to be seeping from the sediments and bottom material long after the initial spill.

Chemical composition and complex environmental factors of a particular marine area make it difficult to generalize about the effects of oil spills. Gasoline and jet fuels will evaporate relatively quickly, leaving behind dead plankton, larvae and localized damage. Mixed petroleum substances such as oils containing different percentages of hydrocarbons will lose lower molecular weight compounds (gasoline) quickly, but the residual substances will concentrate toxins, change in specific gravity and, depending on conditions, sink to the bottom affecting other species.

Oil spilled in the marine environment is acted upon by natural forces causing it to dissolve, evaporate, oxidize or biodegrade. Biodegradation of petroleum spills occurs by the action of bacteria. There are about seventy species of microscopic bacteria that eat hydrocarbons. These bacteria are known as petrophiles.

One of the most significant observations of bacterial action on oil spills is that the organisms prefer straight chain alkanes and avoid or only very slowly degrade aromatics of higher molecular weight. These high molecular weight aromatics, as we've indicated, are the most toxic. Thus while present research leaves many questions unanswered, the result of this natural degrading process could, theoretically at least, render the substances left in the marine environment more toxic. Some researchers have developed super-eaters, bacterial strains that will eat a wide variety of hydrocarbons. A private enterprise even manufactures and sells bacteria in a dried powder base to be spread on oil-contaminated water to speed up the degrading process.

Biodegradation by these bacteria will not occur in anerobic conditions. Petroleum products settled in the sediment can only be acted upon if there is some means of stirring the bottom to get the compounds into suspension. In the case of number 2 fuel oil, containing 40% aromatic hydrocarbons, it has been established that spillage in an area of little bottom mixing where the sedimentation has occurred will require fifteen years to rejuvenate sufficiently to support marine life, especially oysters. If there is no action that removes these substances from the sediments, then the oil spills will have long-term adverse effects on the ecology.

Studies made on oil spills have shown that oysters removed from their contaminated beds and replanted in clean circulating water have taken eight months to purge themselves of hydrocarbons. Carcinogens, however, were found to accumulate in the oyster tissue.

At first blush, the mechanical or physical damage resulting from a petroleum spill seems the most damaging aspect of the accident. While the short-term effects are more drastic, the long-term aspects of petroleum discharges, dumping, or spills, are extremely dangerous to the marine ecology.

Research into the effects of petroleum spills on the marine or estuarial environment has only recently become a priority item. Now, those who use, refine, ship, or store petroleum must, as part of permitting requirements, provide environmental impact studies as to the potential effect spills, if they occur, will have on aquatic life. This new research resulted in the discovery of dynamic ecological factors that are still not completely understood. What is clear is that petroleum dumping and spillage in the ocean has, is and will take a toll not limited to the organisms killed directly. There will be residual damage over time as well as human poisonings resulting in disease or accumulation in the human food chain of disease-causing substances.

Horrible mistakes have been made by well-intentioned attempts to clean up petroleum spills using solvents, chemical dispersants, and sundry materials. These chemicals react with the oil, changing the way the new mixture affects marine life. The synergistic effects of solvent-oil mixtures have been disasterous. The solvent has often increased the oil product's ability to enter the organisms' tissues, giving it solubility it never before had.

Some chemical dispersants are preferred as food by petrophilic bacteria, which feed off the chemicals and leave the oil. It has been found that some petrophilic bacteria preferred the substances that were spread on the water to trap the oil and cause it to settle to the bottom. *Craie de champagne* (chalk powder) is a very effective settling agent. Its use in Britanny, France compounded the oil-spill problem by offsetting the important natural forces that degrade the oil. The bacteria prefer eating the chalk, and the settling of the oil prevented evaporation, leaving long-term residual sediments.

The world's recoverable offshore crude oil reserves have been estimated at 160 thousand million barrels. More than 14 million million cubic meters of natural gas are potentially recoverable from undersea sources. As of 1972, a total of approximately 5.5 thousand million barrels of oil and some 680 thousand million cubic meters of gas were recovered from areas off the shores of the United States. In the world, in 1972, about 3.5 thousand million barrels of oil and 184 thousand million cubic meters of gas were taken from beneath the seas. Since 1960, there has been a 9% per year increase in the transport of oil by tanker ships. There were no offshore oil platforms off the United States in 1948. Now there are 4,500.

All of these statistics increase the inevitable likelihood of pollution by oil spills. Quite obviously, mankind has and will more vigorously pursue exploration of these valuable oil reserves. Inevitably, in that pursuit man will wantonly, carelessly, involuntarily, even sorrowfully diminish the ability of the oceans to sustain life.

Lamentable maritime disasters resulting in massive petroleum spills into the ocean environment have left behind names that will live in infamy. Tanker disasters like the *Amoco Cadiz*, wrecked on the rocks off Brittany's coast, spilled millions of gallons of oil into the waters of France's prime fishing and shellfishing waters, destroying as well the summer tourist industry. The *Torrey Canyon* crashed upon the Seven Stones rocks off Cornwall, England in March 1967, spilling some 850,000 barrels of crude oil into the sea, destroying Britain's summer tourist industry and devastating marine resources.

Offshore oil rigs which, on the whole, have excellent statistical safety records, become the focus of sensational publicity when an accident does occur. The blowout of the *Ixtoc 1* well in Campeche Bay, fifty miles offshore in the Gulf of Mexico, has spilled about 2.5 million barrels of oil into the Gulf. The *Ixtoc 1* well blowout spewed uncontrolled for months, spilling oil over a 600-mile length of Texas Gulf Coast beaches.

Everywhere oil was seen on the surface, tests made by researchers discovered it beneath the surface as well. Some samples taken from Gulf waters, revealed that the *Ixtoc 1* oil was beneath the surface, as deep as 65 feet. Much of this oil washed ashore in the midst of the tourist season, turning away business. The Campeche Bay well blowout provoked international claims for reparations from the United States against the Mexican Government, with counterclaims by the Mexicans that the United States did not compensate them for changing the salinity of the water in the Gulf which adversely affected the Mexican fishing industry.

While these drastic accidents occur and will continue to occur in conformity with actuarial statistics, the day-to-day spillage and dumping of petroleum products in the oceans and waterways consistently poses a vital perennial threat.

Coast Guard figures show, for example, that in the first six months of 1979, there were 137 separate spills of oil and chemicals in excess of 50 gallons each in the waters of the Delaware Bay and River and the south Jersey and Delaware shore. This accounted for a total spillage of 64,612 gallons, representing an increase of 160% from the 25,000 gallons spilled in the last half of 1978. In the upper Hudson River Valley, the Coast Guard logged spillage of 15,428 gallons of oil and hazardous chemicals in 29 separate incidents during the first half of 1979—an increase of 4,000 gallons over the 11,717 gallons spilled in the same area during the last half of 1978.

Statistics compiled by the Coast Guard for Long Island Sound in the first half of 1979, showed that there were 84 separate spills, totaling 24,679 gallons of oil and chemicals. This was an increase of 16,000 gallons over the amount spilled in the Sound during the last six months of 1978.

In New York Harbor, the six month Coast Guard figures for 1979 show that 338,725 gallons of oil and chemicals entered the harbor waters. These figures were tabulated for 89 separate spill incidents and were almost 50% higher than these pollution spills in the same area during the last half of 1978.

While it is imprudent to leap to hasty conclusions from limited statistical analyses, it is fair to assume that the impact of oil spills and chemical dumping directly into the oceans and via rivers, harbors and waterways is increasing and will continue to increase with increases in activities demanding and creating demand for petroleum products. What is also apparent is that the cumulative effects of this dumping or spilling of pollutants into the oceans will have profound effects upon the quality of life in the future. The consequences will be far more serious than a bather's inconvenience by tar balls washing up on beaches hundreds, perhaps thousands of miles from where the oil spill occurred.

THERMAL DISCHARGES AND OTHER POLLUTION FROM POWER PLANTS

Marine organisms are very sensitive to fluctuations in water temperature. For some fish, warming water temperature is a signal to spawn. If the signal is a false one, then the animal will lay eggs at a time or in a manner where the young cannot survive. Cyclical changes in the temperature affect the bloom of marine plants. Increasing the temperature of the water, as in the normal summer season, means an increase in algal bloom.

While there are many uncontrollable factors in the natural environment, creatures have adapted to a regular cycle of seasonal changes which support life. When man alters the natural environment, then the natural clock is adversely affected. Such has been the case with the construction and operation of large nuclear and fossil-fuel power plants, which, often built along the ocean or its tributaries, use water to cool reactor elements, discharing it at a much elevated temperature.

Warm water is able to retain less oxygen than cold, but the many more subtle ecological relationships that exist in a given ecosphere near the power plants have only recently come under scrutiny. Power plants not only discharge heated waste water but, as part of their antifouling maintenance, add chlorine to eliminate fungus and bacteria which build up on the plants' condensing tubes. Fossil-fuel power plants, reverting to coal as a source of cheap power in the energy crisis, add heavy metals to the environment as a result of coal ash being released from holding ponds. The coal ash thus released not only contains sulfur, copper, zinc, arsenic, selenium, and chromium, but changes the pH of the water. Coal ash discharge can also create silt which suffocates marine organisms.

Permits are now required by law in order for a power plant to discharge waste, including "thermal discharges." While permitting requires demonstration of environmental soundness, the results of biological testing to date provide insufficient evidence to be able to judge the effects of all of the dynamic pollution factors associated with thermal discharges. Even now, scientists are building artificial test streams and exposing marine organisms in the laboratory to various aspects of pollution. To what extent the collective effects are synergistic, having a greater total adverse environmental effect acting together than the sum of the harm when acting alone, is still unknown. For example, in warmer water fish are affected by poisons in the water

131

to a greater degree than the same fish living in cold water. Two factors may thus combine, the toxins and the thermal discharge, to kill the fish.

Thermal discharges are probably the most well researched of the effects power plants have on the marine environment. Still, the issue is debated, with the environmentalists on the one hand calling the heated waste water "thermal pollution" and the power plant technicians on the other calling it "thermal enrichment."

Elevating the water temperature increases certain of the nutrients in the water. Fish living in the area of the thermal discharge will have an increased metabolism rate, therefore consuming more food. Some creatures thrive in the warmer water resulting from power plant discharges. Other forms of life are adversely affected. Since the temperature differences may be as much as $20°F$, this can permanently alter the character and composition of the environment. In one example, thermal discharge studies have shown that shrimp in an area did not tolerate higher temperatures, while sea nettles thrived in the warmer water.

Ecological changes resulting from alteration in the physical marine environment have barely been discovered, let alone understood. The cumulative effects of pollution resulting from power plant discharges are complex, touching on the life cycles and health of a wide variety of organisms. Technology is being developed to run water through cooling towers before it is discharged to minimize the thermal effects on the marine environment. Fuel shortages are forcing utilities to return to the use of coal, even high-sulfur-content coal. If the environmental problems cannot adequately be resolved, the cumulative effects may result in destruction and disruption in the natural balance on a grand scale.

DETERGENTS AND EUTROPHICATION

The word eutrophication is derived from the Greek words eutrophos which means well nourished and trephein, to nourish. Eutrophication is a word used to describe an aquatic condition where there is a blooming of algal growth. Many conditions, natural and man-made, may contribute to this algal bloom, eventually causing an imbalance in the marine environment.

In an abnormal situation, the organisms which normally feed off the algae cannot consume the large numbers produced, so the excess algae die in the water. Algae, like all plants, produce oxygen through photosynthesis by day. Algae consume oxygen when photosynthesis ceases at night. The dead algae are decomposed by bacteria. As the dead algae increase, so do the bacteria. In the process of using the algae for food, these bacteria also consume oxygen. Thus, as the cycle progresses, oxygen is depleted and higher forms of life are either smothered or leave the area for water richer in oxygen.

In nature, algal blooms can be cyclical. There are numerous examples, however, where man-made pollutants have contributed to imbalances and thus have created massive kills of invertebrate and fish life. These environmental disruptions have resulted in situations where oxygen was depleted and eutrophication occurred. As discussed, elevated water temperatures from thermal discharges have often been the cause of algal blooms resulting in eutrophication of water resources. Sewage discharges have likewise been responsible for triggering this destructive process. Increased nutrients in the water, often the by-products of man's waste, have also accounted for widespread algal growth.

Phosphates and sulfonates are plant nutrients. They are also products that have been widely used in laundry detergents. Since these phosphates and sulfonates do not degrade in the waste water treatment process, the nutrient-rich detergent waste reaches streams, lakes, rivers, and oceans as effluent from sewage discharges. The algae triggered by increased nutrients, bloom in proportions that cannot be handled in the normal food chain. Eventually, in the process of eutrophication, these algal blooms deprive higher animal forms of oxygen, resulting in massive fish kills, if the fish cannot escape to clean water, and invertebrate kills.

THE RED TIDE

The words "Red Tide" provoke environmental concern, drawing to mind thousands of dead fish and closed bathing beaches. A red tide is caused by a bloom or proliferation of tiny dinoflagellates. These tiny creatures, one-celled marine plants with two flagella that enable them to move three dimensionally, may reach 60,000,000 per liter of sea water. These dinoflagellates turn the water reddish brown as they consume the nutrients. In death and decay, they cause depletion of the oxygen in the water, causing massive fish kills.

Gonyaulax, one kind of dinoflagellate, produces a toxin. This poison can enter man's food chain through the tissue of mussels and clams. Human deaths resulting from eating shellfish contaminated with dinoflagellate toxin have been reported in cold water areas. Deaths have occurred in Belgium, and red tides in waters off England and Germany have disproved the notion that they occur only in tropical water.

Sewage dumping has been blamed for red tides, but a natural upwelling of nutrients can also be responsible. Red tides have, in fact, been reported in areas before sewage dumping occurred.

In any upwelling or proliferation of nutrients in the sea, the phytoplankton, such as diatoms, also proliferate. Dinoflagellates show up to feed, coming with a special advantage: the dinoflagellates enjoy a moveable feast, propelling toward the surface sunlight or deeper for any source of food that occurs there. As in the case with most imbalances, red tide damage occurs when the dinoflagellates consume most of the usable oxygen in the water. In the process of putrefication, suffocation of other organisms results. Toxins emitted in the putrefication process also kill marine organisms. Cases of human poisonings from toxin-contaminated shellfish have also been reported.

PHYSICAL ALTERATIONS AND DAMAGE

"We have become a sorcerer's apprentice on a grand scale," Taghi Farvar said in a compendium of technical environmental papers he edited, published under the title *The Careless Technology*. Man, in attempting to adjust nature, according to Farvar, has created unintended environmental backlash. Adjustments here and there have sometimes created countermeasures in nature, compensating for the imbalances created by man.

Huge dams and massive canal projects have undone many of the environmental checks and balances that have preserved the balance of nature over centuries, and with that balance the traditional human way of life for people living in the area. Many of these dam and canal projects have resulted in adverse effects on the marine environment. These untoward and unwanted side effects, instead of bringing prosperity and wealth, in the long run have degenerated human health and ocean resources. More and more we are discovering that in the natural scheme of things, subtleties play an important role, not only in the food chain, but in physical conditions that support higher forms of life. When man alters one aspect of his environment, usually for some presumed human benefit, the act may provoke other events or a chain reaction of changes that may, as far as man is concerned, wipe out any potential benefit created by his adjusting nature in the first place.

Taghi Farvar's comments above were applicable to the Aswan Dam project in Egypt. Traditional nutrient-rich mud no longer flowed to fertilize crops below the dam causing consternation among land farmers. The mud and silt backed up into the sea, causing disruption in the Egyptian fishing, changing patterns of behavior and territorial traditions that had been the subsistence of fishermen in the area for centuries.

Each time a ship passes through the Panama Canal, 52 million gallons of fresh water flow into the sea coming from Gatun Lake in the middle of the Isthmus. Fifteen thousand ships pass through the canal each year. This accounts for massive ecological changes. Fresh-water draw downs come from man-made lakes, part of a large watershed area in the tropical forest. The existence of the canal itself has been jeopardized by excessive deforestation and timber harvesting in the Panama rain forests, watershed land for the fresh-water lakes that enable navigation. In about twenty-five years, 250,000 acres have been denuded of trees, diminishing the watershed of 35% of its protective cover. This has caused floods and runoffs and has diminished the water table of the two lakes, Lake Gatun, the lake in the middle ships must pass through and Lake Alajuela, a lake that feeds water into Lake Gatun. As Lake Gatun dropped, larger ships could not pass through, and in one short period, the lake dropped 3.1 feet below the draft lines of the larger ships. Clearly, the timbering has had a profound effect on the water table. Silting is evident in the lakes, and even as the United States relinquished control of the Panama Canal, the developers continued to harvest the forests and develop the watershed. The continued sedimentation will program the demise of the canal, and with its demise a major impact on world commerce will be felt—an example of the natural interrelationships between the land and water resources, including changes in the normal 3.5 % salinity of the oceans.

Regrettable physical damage has been done to our coral reefs. So incensed is Bill Crawford, one of Key Largo's best-known dive charter captains, at the damage being done to Florida's offshore reefs by reckless anchoring that he will insist boatmen reanchor where he sees their chains are breaking coral. Physical breakage is everywhere in Pennekamp Park, the result of improper or careless anchoring.

PERSPECTIVE ON GREED AND POLLUTION

"The problem of the pollution of New York Harbor by sewage and

135

factory wastes is perennial...the Aquarium staff is perhaps more painfully aware of the harbor situation than most persons, since the conditions have had such a direct bearing on its problems. Originally the marine tanks were piped direct to the harbor and the mortality of the specimens was tremendous," the report stated, in rather familiar terms. The report went on to state what scientists found, "No longer does piling become invested in a coat of living organisms, such as black mussels, etc. Usually only a thin coat of some struggling green algae is present. So bad has the pollution become that a continual production of hydrogen sulphide gas is given off, and, escaping into the atmosphere, pollutes that too. On some days it is strong enough to be readily detected by smell." These excerpts were taken from an article in the *Bulletin of the New York Zoological Society*, the January-February 1938 edition. The article logged the observations of the Society's Aquarium collection boat scientists, documenting the existence of 129 species of fish in the harbor area and bay. A 1926 list enumerated 261 species. The *Bulletin* article concludes, "It is difficult to guess what fishing conditions might be like today if the harbor and river were thoroughly cleaned up. Of this much we may be certain: the invertebrate fauna, now merely obsolete, would certainly be expected to return, and with it such fishes as feed on sessile growths." The list of fishes in this 1938 article, if published today, would more likely serve as an obituary column than a checklist, yet the results were clearly predicted and predictable as this published article attests.

We have discussed the great arribadas of nesting sea turtles in the Yucatan. A 1947 Kodak Pathe film records an arribada on the beach of Rancho Nuevo. It shows 40,000 Kemp's ridley turtles coming ashore to nest. This year, maybe 400 to 500 ridleys nested on Rancho Nuevo beach, maybe less. Man has left a wake as he crashed through nature—overharvesting, waste, depletion, pollution, destruction. It has been such a wide swath of abuse in such a short period of time that many effects have not caught up with the causes; but they will. When the extent of harm done to the ocean environment is finally known, the realization may come too late to reverse the trend. Future generations may be doomed to an austerity that probably can be avoided only if people of all nations recognize the oceans as resources belonging to the world and unite to preserve them.

9

The Oceans as Vessels for Commerce and Civilization

He lived in the fo'c'sle, crowded in with his fellow "sons of adversity and calamity." Shipmates, a word that compels in definition imagery of a rugged existence. Men huddled together, bending halliards, reefing canvas before the mast. Herman Melville understood the hardship of life at sea and wrote about it as many other seafaring authors did; with respect, awe, with love and hatred.

Modern counterparts of Melville's "sons of adversity and calamity," do not today suffer the privations of long two or three year voyages away from home nor endure corporal punishment for breach of ironclad ship's discipline. Computer steering systems, automation and modern navigational aids notwithstanding, in 1978 some 41.2% of the seamen aboard American flag vessels reported job related shipboard injuries.

I've poured over archives and early documentary photographs for many ports. Looking at the tall masts, bowsprits jutting over the foot of New York's South Street, I wondered how there was room to walk about. Quays bustling with wagons, men, and horses hauling and shifting cargo, dense thickets of rigging spanning the waterfront with webs.

I walked the docks pictured in many of these old daguerrotypes, dismayed that so many of the piers have fallen into disuse and decay.

Last Christmas I mailed my cards to Europe early, using surface mail. The cards were returned to me with a notation by the postal service: "No winter steamship service to Europe." Since the U.S. Mail must be carried in U.S. flagships, this apparently meant there were no American sailings to Europe. It couldn't be, I thought. It was not possible. As a result, I became more attentive to the Times shipping and sailing notices.

The bankruptcy of the Pacific Far East Lines in 1978 left only eight American subsidized flag steamship carriers in operation. Even with large government subsidies, of the eight remaining merchant marine lines, three are operating in the red. Five other flag carriers are barely surviving with only marginal operations.

After World War II, the United States was first in merchant shipping. Today, the U.S. is in tenth place and losing ground rapidly. When the Pacific Far East Lines built their last ship in 1976, it was constructed with $40.4 million in government money. Over the next three years, the Pacific Far East Lines received $70.3 million in U.S. government subsidies until their bankruptcy in 1978. The poor condition of American merchant shippping has prompted a member of the U.S. House of Representative's Merchant Marine Committee to declare that these extensive government subsidies "have failed to halt the chronic decay of the American shipbuilding and merchant marine industries."

Much of the cargo shipped into and out of the Ports of New York and New Jersey is carried in foreign flagships. Statistics reveal that about 300,000 seamen of all nationalities put into the Port of New York each year, with more than 3500 ships from all countries docking annually at Port Newark's container ship piers. According to the most reliable calculations I could find, the yearly cost for shipping freight over the oceans is $16 billion.

In the early days, when harbors around America's port cities bustled with trade, American clipper captains vied to break speed records. Ships' chandlers rushed to outfit and refit the sleek windships that brought American commerce and industry to the far reaches of the world.

America's decline as a nation reliant upon its own ocean commerce is only symbolic. That symbolism is most vividly expressed by the decay and deterioration of many of our waterfronts and harbors, a decline in shipbuilding and, in some cases, abandonment of ocean commerce to other nations entirely. When one nation declines in maritime power, the slack will be taken up by others quick to realize the importance of a strong merchant marine.

While whimsical national attitudes shift, while various factors influence a country's economic policy of putting ships upon the sea, there remains a certain spirit inherent in seafaring that defies defeat. Part of that human spirit is adventure, part discovery, part an indefinable sense that has meant men will go to sea because it is part of their empirical being.

Historically, the Marshall islanders, plying vast reaches of the Pacific in dugout canoes with outriggers, had only the sun, the stars, currents and winds to guide them. With a sense for reading these elements, the island people spread their civilization across thousands of miles of ocean. Stick charts served as the Marshallese navigators' memory of the currents and winds. They served to teach children the art of navigation. Shells, marking islands, were attached to the charts. Wave patterns were shown with sticks. Subtle changes in the ocean that would go unnoticed by ordinary navigators were indicated on the stick charts. They are only souvenirs now, sold at the airstrip to tourists that pass through on their way somewhere else. For the most part they are overlooked, overshadowed by hand-woven baskets or ships models. To the Marshallese, these stick charts symbolize their civilization.

No one knows the origin of the Polynesian people with any degree of certainty. Anthropologists guess that Polynesians migrated from Indonesia or the Malayan archipelago. It is believed that these people set out across the Pacific two hundred years before Christ was born. Their boats probably changed very little over the centuries. Now the great Polynesian outriggers are only used for ceremonial purposes.

These early Polynesian navigators named many stars. They differentiated between the planets and the stars, calling some of the planets magical names, recognizing that planets change position in the heavens. Venus was called Naholoholo in Polynesian. Roughly interpreted, it meant running back and forth in the heavens. Realizing that stars, not planets, held a truer plot was an early navigational sophistication. It was probably by holding on the star Sirius, that these early explorers discovered Tahiti. From Tahiti, the star Arcturus likely guided these adventurous seafarers to discover the Hawaiian Islands at a time when the Roman civilization was in decline.

The ordered and resilient Polynesians settled the Australian isles in the fourteenth century. Their Maori culture flourished until the age of exploration and discovery in the nineteenth century.

I stood at Venus Point on the Island of Tahiti, by a small cove where Captain Cook was said to have first come ashore. A child was swimming in the coral lagoon; an older woman was combing her hair with Monoi oil made from pleasantly scented flowers. It was the Monoi, carried on the wind, that gave early sailors a whiff of sweetness blowing offshore long before they set eyes on land. The tiny cove and placid beach were abandoned except for the woman and little child; back from the beach, nets were set to dry by fishermen. Anyone who doubts the lure of the sea should stand in that quiet cove at Venus Point. The Polynesians felt this special magnetism of the oceans. It drew them to these islands two thousand years ago.

Polynesian civilization is linked to the sea. It surrounds their being on every side. For the whole of their lives, these people are but a few steps from her shores.

We are all as dependent upon the sea today as the early Polynesians were. This influence transcends worlds and draws one nation into another as surely and as strongly as it drew early Polynesians to discover Tahiti and early Vikings to conquer the mysteries of the Atlantic.

There is a special oneness with the sea, a spirit fiction writers know. Riding in the bows of a speeding ship, navigating the passes and reefs at night with a Tahitian friend, I had little doubt of this special relationship with the sea. The boat's sails were replaced with a powerful outboard engine, its tiller with a steering wheel. The intense eyes of the pilot, his gaze cutting through the night, navigating us home through treacherous reefs, linked two civilizations and two centuries. The Pacific was the cradle of this man's civilization, the sea's bounty provided life itself. More, it provided independence and freedom.

The Mediterranean, it has been said, was the cradle of modern civilization, touching the borders of Greece, Rome, Tyre, Phoenicia, Egypt; great ancient cultures that give us our heritage.

In Cairo's museum, ships with sails are pictured on vases turned earlier than 2600 B.C. A battle of ships is depicted in a mural on the tomb of Ramses III, painted around 1200 B.C.

Arab dhows have changed very little in design over time. Some are now equipped with diesel engines, but Arab traders still ply the coast as they have for centuries, stopping to trade at ports along the Red Sea. Watching sailors load sacks of grain and trade goods aboard these wooden dhows, one has the impression that time stood still.

Flying low over the Red Sea, I saw Arab dhows navigating the coast, probably in much the same way as they did in the time of the Pharaohs. Lateen sails were innovations, originally copied from Arab dhows. These triangular sheets enabled ships to sail close to the wind more efficiently than square sails.

From the Island of Crete, the Minoans conquered the Athenians, dominating the Mediterranean with powerful naval forces. A succession of powers followed the Minoans. The Phoenicians, sailing from the port of Tyre, were great navigators and explorers. Herodotus wrote that the Phoenicians sailed around the world.

A modern day explorer, treasure diver Bob Marx, had been trying to locate the remains of a Phoenician ship in North America. Every time someone reports they have discovered the remains of a wreck resembling a Phoenician ship, Bob sets off, hoping to prove the theory that the Phoenicians were the first to discover America. So far all of Bob's leads have been unproductive. He persists in the hope that some day he will discover evidence of the Phoenician discovery of America. When political conditions permit and it becomes possible to dive off Tyre again, Bob Marx plans to return to learn what he can about Phoenician shipwrecks. Bob's dream is to build a replica of a Phoenician ship and sail it from the Mediterranean across the Atlantic, proving the theory of Phoenician discovery.

Roman civilization depended on the sea. Their vessels carried commerce to far flung reaches of the empire. One Roman innovation, a huge gangway that could be lowered over an enemy ship, was a precursor to the use of marines. This tactic enabled Romans to defeat the Carthaginians.

Scuba divers take navigation for granted. Our dive boats proceed to the site with pinpoint accuracy using loran, a radio navigation device that enables a pilot to return to the same spot in the ocean. Radio beacons emit signals, interpreted as digits on a screen. Radar enables a pilot to navigate blind in any weather. Radar is now standard equipment, but there are gentle reminders that it is only a recent innovation.

Recently, a skipper of a police launch in New York Harbor reminisced about the days when he first came on the job, some twenty years before. The patrol boats did not have radar. "Wooden boats. Boy were they cold in winter. We would run compass courses across the harbor in the fog. Each man would have his own courses worked out. If we saw something coming, we'd divert. You couldn't see anything in a fog," the police pilot explained. "We'd come to a bridge and know it by the condensation dripping off. Then we'd follow the drips of condensation across to the other side, couldn't even see the bridge, fog gets so thick. Things were certainly different when I came to work here," the harbor policeman remarked, sentimental about the old, wondering how they ever did without the new navigational aids.

Things were indeed different. Divers take such things as loran, radar, sonar, and recording fathometers for granted. Many of these devices have only been invented and developed with the advent of scuba, around the time of World War II.

Sonar aids in shipwreck location. A device, lowered through the ship's hull, emits a sound which goes out in the water until it strikes an object, then bounces back. A skilled charter captain can read these patterns on a screen or chart and be able to locate wrecks on the bottom. When an object is found, a recording fathometer can develop the object's profile on a screen.

These inventions, while adapted by divers to their special purposes, have also vastly improved commercial navigation upon the sea. Even the yellow plastic compass scuba enthusiasts strap to their wrists to navigate underwater is a sophisticated improvement over the instruments early explorers had to find their way across vast oceans.

We often ask charter captains what speed the dive boat is making and are given an answer in knots. It was actually only in the seventeenth century that a means was devised to measure a ship's speed. The feat was first accomplished by lowering a board over the side attached to a line. The line was knotted at spaced intervals. The line was payed out against sand in a glass. The number of knots that passed overboard indicated the ship's speed. The tally was recorded in a log. This system accounts for today's use of knots and log books.

The sea is a way of life in Hong Kong. Anchorages with romantic names such as Aberdeen, Run Away Bay, Stanley, conjure up adventurous seafaring tales. In Aberdeen alone there are usually more than 4000 ships rafted together. More than one hundred thousand people live aboard junks, crowded together in Hong Kong's anchorages. Walking along narrow alleys and passages in Aberdeen, the impression of dependence on the sea is everywhere.

Fishing junks, nets drying on hoists, sell their catch as quickly as it is landed. Around the harbor, men and women in simple wooden skiffs catch fish and shellfish. Fish mongers are everywhere, scaling and cutting fish as Chinese housewives shop the evening's meal.

In Thailand there is a different culture, but the impression is the same. Squid are dried, prized as food. Everything taken from the sea is

*For the fishermen at Sattahip on Thailand's coast, fishing means survival. The catch is sorted at
the end of the day, then salted and dried.*

used for human consumption. The rivers and waterways are vital to
national survival. River taxis and klong boats zip along bringing
commuters to and from work; shoppers to and from market. The Thai
civilization is dependent on the sea and water resources flowing to it.

Perhaps the closer one lives to nature, the greater the dependence
on the ocean and its tributaries. This focus becomes more apparent in
lesser-developed countries.

For many days I navigated the Congo River in what is now Zaire.
The trip went from what was then called Stanley Falls to Stanley
Pool. The river boat was not only a source of transportation, but a
vital part of commerce. Fishermen from tribes along the river would
paddle out and catch hold of the river boat as it passed. Traders on
board the river boat would throw colored cloths into the wooden
fishing pirogues, bidding on immense river catfish.

When the fishing boats were tied alongside, the fishermen and
traders would barter for the fish. The fishermen would buy supplies
they needed. The traders would ice the catfish, for sale at a great profit
when the river boat docked at the capital. The Congo River was the

143

center of commerce for tribes of people, even the inhabitants of the capital.

Unusual sights, strange to foreign eyes, filled each glance along the river portage. Crocodiles were hoisted aboard. They were alive, tied to stakes until they arrived at the capital, where they would be butchered for food. Smoked crocodile meat hung from the bullwarks, awaiting delivery at market. The river was life. Its flow of nutrients washed down from the tropical rain forests in the interior enriched the ocean which supported offshore fishing.

The seas and oceans, the tributaries and rivers, are intertwined with the entire natural ecology. Historically this meant that civilization developed around the sea. Water transport remains the only practical means of commerce, and commerce is national strength. This has been so over the history of mankind. It will continue, perhaps even more significantly, as the oceans become man's last frontier.

10

So Shall We Reap in the Oceans

The future of the oceans is being contemplated by world diplomats attempting to work out a treaty establishing new parameters for the Law of the Sea. While these United Nations Conferences on the Law of the Sea have been fitful and often disappointing, frequently breaking down over such issues as who would sit where at a conference table, there is a recognition of the importance of ocean resources for the future of mankind. There is also recognition that ocean pollution, destruction, and depletion transcends national boundaries and must be solved on an international level.

One aspect of working on conservation issues that is most surprising is that many of today's problems were recognized years ago as threats which could cause grave health or environmental damage. Ample documentation exists, written and reported by courageous and far-sighted people who not only described the problems, but analyzed the potential for future harm. The authors of the 1938 *Zoological Society Bulletin*, discussed earlier, for example, described the decline of fish species in lower New York Bay as the result of pollution.

Diving companions who have devoted their lives to the sea, for as long as I can remember, have been telling me about problems resulting from dumping toxic material in the oceans. These friends have been going to town meetings to protest ocean dumping. The same companions have urged me, for as long as I've known them, to write about ocean environment issues in articles I do for magazines, so that people would know what was happening.

When one of my first magazine articles dealing with ocean pollution was published, I discussed it with my diving friends. I recall that while none of them disputed the facts, the majority were just not particularly interested in the issues. Recently at a diving seminar where I spoke on ocean environment problems, I was surrounded by divers after the talk, persons seeking additional information.

Students I teach in basic diving classes are increasingly more aware of environmental problems. Their questions, interest, and dedication to preserving and conserving ocean resources are only exceeded by their enthusiasm for diving.

Even though many citizens are concerned about conservation, it is often difficult to obtain government regulation that will compel business responsibility. It is more difficult to obtain international consensus.

The United Nations Law of the Sea Conference has been trying to hammer out a comprehensive treaty since 1974. No agreement has been reached, prompting Ambassador T.B. Koh of Singapore to declare that "a Conference failure would be a disaster for the world community, leading to chaos on the seas and conflicts over resources."

One of the issues at the conference is a 200-mile national economic zone. To get some conception of the effect a 200-mile control zone would have, one only has to shade in a map of the world. Shaded areas, drawn to scale, two hundred miles from every sea coast and island, make the impact apparent. Ocean straits and corridors would fall within the parochial control of nations. Without international agreement, nations exercising control over a 200-mile zone could effectively prevent passage over the seas and block ocean commerce.

The major issues being considered by the U.N. Conference on the Law of the Sea concern territorial seas and straits, the 200-mile economic zone, fisheries, international seabeds, marine pollution, and scientific research. Related issues concern methods of settling disputes, the regime of islands, landlocked countries and geographically disadvantaged states, control of the high seas beyond the 200-mile zone, and miscellaneous problems associated with the major issues.

The probable final resolution of the issue of territorial rights over the oceans will be to increase territorial waters from 3 to 12 miles

146

with treaty provisions providing for the unimpeded passage through straits used for international navigation. There will likely also be international accord accepting a 200-mile economic zone. This 200-mile economic zone will mean that coastal states would have exclusive rights to explore and exploit living and nonliving resources within that zone. The United States position at the Law of the Sea Conference, on the 200-mile economic zone issue, would require coastal states to enforce international pollution standards, insure noninterference with other uses of the ocean (such as navigation and scientific research), and agree to be bound by dispute settlement mechanisms. U.S. delegates favored a position allowing foreign fishing within the coastal states 200-mile control zone for that portion of the allowable catch that a coastal state could not itself harvest. It is also clear that control of fisheries within the 200-mile zone will be used as a political weapon as was done by the President, restricting Soviet fishing off U.S. waters after the invasion of Afghanistan.

The U.N. General Assembly resolved that the oceans beyond the limits of national jurisdiction should be the common heritage of mankind. In spite of this postulate, the U.N. Law of the Sea treaty has been stalled by national self-interests regarding ocean resources and extensive bickering over who gets what share of the seabed.

As science and technology improve, man's exercise of power over ocean resources will increase. If international responsibility does not also increase, the oceans will lose. All mankind will lose in this scrambling for wealth under the seas.

A recent article proclaimed the headline: "Possible Tuna War With Canada." This resulted from a notice in the Federal Register prohibiting the entry of all Canadian tuna products into the United States. The cause of this action was the seizure of eight U.S. tuna fishing boats, 56 miles off Canada's West coast. Canada claims a 200-mile control zone over tuna and enforced it by seizing U.S. fishing boats. Under Federal law, when the Secretary of State certifies the unjustified seizure of an American fishing vessel, the U.S. Customs Service then must prohibit the entry into the U.S. of any of the offending country's fish exports. Since tuna is a migratory fish, U.S. officials have been pressing for international agreement to regulate tuna fishing.

There are complicated laws that govern import duties on fish. If a country gives its fishermen "bounties or grants," thus making the prices they can charge too favorable as against the price U.S. fishermen charge, then the U.S. Treasury Department can increase

147

customs duties on imports to make the price competitive.

In a case involving Canadian bounties and grants to fishermen, the International Trade Commission forstalled a crisis by declaring there was no injury to the U.S. fishing industry. The Treasury Department decided that while Canada granted favorable bounties to its fishermen, the U.S. would not levy duties on their imports.

It is clear that there are many political factors that influence and affect various uses of the oceans and ocean resources. Disputes such as those that arose between two close neighbors, friends and allies, the United States and Canada, emphasize the importance of reaching an international understanding. A mechanism for the peaceful settlement of disputes over ocean issues is a world imperative. Armed gunboats seizing crews and ships can provoke an international incident leading to an aggravated military situation, even tempt warfare between nations.

We are beginning to discover the oceans as we discovered the New World. As mankind pushed terrestrial discovery westward, in only a

A SCUBA diver points to a small flamingo tongue cowrie on a piece of gorgonian coral. These cowries eat the living polyps of the coral. They are often sought by shell collectors, prized for their beauty.

short period of time herds of animals were decimated, and the face of a magnificent continent was left scarred and abused.

Divers are today's pioneers. We have probed the ocean in primitive diving dress, fragile bodies barely protected from the harsh environment, like those who plied the trail west in moccasin and deerskin jacket. In the very few years since diving has been undertaken with modern technology, in almost the same manner as the pioneers traded pack mules for steam locomotives, we have sent great steel probes into the sea to view and recover her wealth. It is progress. Progress requires responsibility; greater responsibility today than ever before.

There are places in the seas and oceans where the diver's presence is not feared. There our intrusion only attracts the curious marine creatures which have not yet known the killing twang of a speargun, the crashing bulldozer of a fishing boat's underwater trawl, the foul stuff of man's manufacturing waste.

We stand together at the water's edge. We stand on the frontier, some of us garbed as pioneers, aquatic counterparts of Americans who before us wore leather stockings and moccasins. Nature can withstand our intrusion. Behind us, however, the outpourings of industry are doing to the sea what has been done to the land.

Hydrostructure alone will not be sufficient to completely protect the ocean's resources from depletion. Building artificial concrete reefs will help develop living resources. Common sense and conservation will extend the ocean's ability to support life.

When I roll backwards off a boat into the ocean, I still feel the thrill of discovery, deep down excitement. The first western trail blazers must have felt a similar sense of pleasure coming upon a crystal clear mountain spring or wilderness river few if any had seen before.

In 1869, Jules Verne, using the person of Captain Nemo, described the captivating spirit of the ocean realm in the following words: "Yes, I love it! The sea is everything. It covers seven-tenths of the terrestrial globe. Its breath is pure and healthy. It is an immense desert, where man is never lonely, for he feels life stirring on all sides. The sea is only the embodiment of a supernatural and wonderful existence...Nature manifests herself in it by her three kingdoms, mineral, vegetable, and animal. The sea is a vast resevoir of Nature...the sea does not belong to despots. Upon its surface men can still exercise unjust laws, fight, tear one another to pieces, and be carried away with terrestrial horrors. But at thirty feet below its level, their reign ceases. Their influence is quenched, and their power disappears. Ah! sir,—live in the bosom of the waters! There only is independence! There I recognize no monsters! There I am free."

This book has voyaged only a few leagues under this great resevoir of Nature. It is here where we end our journey, encouraging others to continue the voyage of discovery, to explore this ocean heritage, and, above all, to help protect what is fast becoming the last wilderness on Earth.

Index